STUDY SKILLS
· OUTLINING ·
STRATEGIES

Mary Mueller

WALCH PUBLISHING

Dedication

To my husband John,
with love

Acknowledgments

The author thanks her husband and children for the time they allowed her to spend writing this book.

The author expresses appreciation for the professional training she received from Dr. Shirley Thomas and Dr. Brownie Kimbrough. The author thanks Dr. John Rothermich for critiquing an earlier version of this manuscript. The author thanks Mr. Joe White and Dr. Joe Lang at Jefferson College for the opportunity to teach reading to high-school students. Finally, the author thanks Dr. Jerry Barber for including her in the Balanced Literacy training for the Sunrise R-9 School District.

About the Author

Mary Elizabeth Mueller is employed as a K–8 librarian/technology director in the St. Louis, Missouri, area. An educator for over 25 years, she has taught English and reading at many levels.

Ms. Mueller holds a B.S.S.E. in English and social studies (John Brown University), an M.S.E. in reading education (University of Central Arkansas), and a M.A. in Library Science (University of Missouri).

1   2   3   4   5   6   7   8   9   10

ISBN 0-8251-4605-4

Copyright © 2004

Walch Publishing

P. O. Box 658 • Portland, Maine 04104-0658

walch.com

Printed in the United States of America

WALCH PUBLISHING

Study Skills Strategies: Outlining
Contents

To the Teacher

Some students seem to know instinctively how to study. They plan their time efficiently, take clear notes, and use effective techniques to review material. Unfortunately, these students are in the minority. Most students need to be taught how to study in order to make good use of their time in school. The *Study Skills Strategies* series teaches students how to read and write efficiently. *Study Skills Strategies: Outlining* shows students how to use outlining as an effective reading strategy by helping them see how structure orders a given text. By analyzing the organization of a selection, students can extract clues that help them process meaning. Understanding the structural pattern of a selection helps readers identify the main idea and its surrounding details.

Study Skills Strategies: Outlining presents common structural designs—process, problem/solution, cause/effect, comparison/contrast, general/specific and definition—as blueprints for the sorting-out process that precedes outlining. Each chapter presents one of these patterns as having a recognizable format, a main idea with a specific function, and distinct linking words. Graphic organizers help students visually recognize individual patterns.

After your students understand the framework of each pattern, they will be able to transform a reading selection into an outlining format. Some students may rely on the graphic organizer to assimilate and understand the overall design. Other students may not need the graphic organizer in constructing outlines. Eventually, both visual and nonvisual learners will become skilled in pattern recognition. They will develop individual reading strategies for understanding and recording informational text.

Used in combination with other reading strategies, such as identifying one's purpose for reading, prereading, scanning, and summarizing, these strategies will help your students become active, effective readers.

Study Skills Strategies: Outlining is easy to use. Each chapter contains reading exercises that you may photocopy as you present that pattern to your class. Chapter 7 contains longer readings and presents a combination of the patterns covered in the previous chapters. Exercises in Chapter 7 focus on a reading strategy that helps students understand individual patterns as components of the integrated pattern. A teacher's guide at the back of the book provides answers to all exercises and general information about the different text structures.

To the Student

We do many different kinds of reading. For pleasure, we might read a novel or a magazine. To learn how to do something, we might read the user manual for a software program. To understand what's going on in the world, we might read a newspaper. Of course, to learn about different subjects in school, we read textbooks.

These different types of reading call for different types of skills. Some reading material is easy to understand; some is harder. Often, the more complex the ideas or information, the harder the material is to read and understand. Luckily, you can learn strategies that will help you with challenging reading. One of these strategies is **outlining**—the subject of this book.

You may already be familiar with one kind of outlining, the kind you do when you are writing an essay. Outlining for writing and outlining for reading are related, but they are also different from each other. When you prepare an outline for writing, you are trying to organize your information in a way that will make sense to your readers. When you prepare an outline from reading, you are recording the important information in the reading passage. Your outline should identify the main ideas and show how they relate to one another. It should give an overview of the information in the reading. In effect, it is an organized way of taking notes. Outlining helps you keep track of what you have already read and how it relates to new information. It also helps you review material without having to read the whole passage again. A good outline can help you keep track of research material for essays. It can also help you review textbook information for tests.

The activities in this book will help you develop outlining skills. You will learn how to identify the main idea in a reading selection. You will also learn to choose the best supporting details to add to your outline. You will see examples of the different ways in which written information is arranged. You will learn when these patterns are likely to be used. Graphic organizers will help you recognize and record each pattern in different outline form.

After a while, you will recognize many different reading patterns. You will have the chance to try many reading strategies, too. Try them all, and find out what works best for you. You may even decide to change some strategies to fit your own way of reading and learning. You may find that you do not need graphic organizers to build outlines. That is fine. With practice, you will spot reading patterns with ease. And you will automatically organize information in the way that is most useful to you.

Recognizing the Pattern

A **process** reading may tell the reader how to do something. It may also describe the way something is done. It is the classic approach of "how-to" writing. The process pattern is quite easy to recognize. You will find this pattern in a set of directions. You can find it in articles that explain how something is done. In school, the process pattern is found often in science textbooks. It is also common in readings for classes like art, technology, driver's education, and physical education.

In the process pattern, information is broken down into a series of steps. Together these steps describe the whole process. Here are some simple examples of the process pattern.

Example 1

The team camping trip involved a lot of effort. First, the team members had to plan meals and buy enough food for a week's stay. Then they had to store the food supply in the team van. Secondly, the team had to load sleeping bags, tents, and other camping equipment into the van. Finally, each member had to wash and pack clothing for hiking, swimming, and mountain-climbing activities.

Process: Getting ready for a team camping trip

Example 2

1. Preheat the oven to 375°F. 2. Measure 1 cup of cake flour. 3. Measure ¾ cup sugar.
4. Measure ¼ teaspoon baking powder. 5. Measure ½ teaspoon salt. 6. Crack 1 egg.
7. Add egg to ¾ cup milk and beat lightly. 8. Mix liquid and dry ingredients together.
9. Grease the pan. 10. Pour the batter into the pan, filling no more than two-thirds full.
11. Bake for 20 minutes, or until the top is golden-brown and springs back when touched.

Process: Baking a cake

Characteristics of the Process Pattern

The process pattern is made up of separate steps that appear in sequence. These steps use action verbs. In **Example 1,** some action verbs are *plan, buy, store, load, wash,* and *pack*.

Look at **Example 2** again. Underline the action verbs.

Major steps within the process pattern often include "ordering" words. In **Example 1,** ordering words include *first*, *then, secondly*, and *finally*.

Look at **Example 2** again. There are no ordering words in this selection. Why do you think this is?

If a reading passage has a series of action steps that are either numbered or joined with ordering words, it is probably an example of a process pattern.

The paragraph in **Example 3** describes a familiar process. We can recognize it as a process because it uses action verbs (*fastened, adjusted, turned on*) and ordering words (*while, then, next, finally*). The paragraph is followed by a line that names the process. Then the steps in the process are listed.

Example 3
The teenagers piled into the car and fastened their seat belts. While they were joking, the driver adjusted the left, right, and rearview mirrors. He then turned on the ignition, checked the driveway for pedestrians, and shifted into reverse. Next, the driver backed the car slowly out of the driveway and turned out into the street, shifted into forward gear, and finally, drove carefully down the road.

Process: Driving a car safely

Process Steps: 1. fastening seat belts

2. adjusting mirrors

3. starting the car

4. checking for pedestrians

5. shifting into reverse

6. backing slowly out of driveway

7. shifting into forward

8. driving carefully down road

The Process Pattern

Once you identify a process pattern in your reading, these strategies can help you read and understand the material:

1. Read the first paragraph carefully. Try to figure out what the process is and where it starts. Skim through the rest of the selection to find the steps of the process.

2. Read the last paragraph carefully. Try to find out where the process ends. If the last paragraph does not give the end of the process, go back one paragraph and check.

3. Read the whole selection. Note the process and its major steps. Key words such as *actions, plans, procedures,* and *steps* can indicate the process pattern. Action verbs usually indicate major steps and substeps. Ordering words such as *first, second, next, then,* and *finally* organize major steps and substeps within the process.

4. Reread the selection. Note any descriptive adjectives and adverbs. Look for verbs that indicate an opinion. These words will help you understand the author's viewpoint. The first and last paragraphs often state and restate the overall process. They also give you an idea of the author's opinion. Read both paragraphs carefully in order to understand the process as the author sees it.

5. Look to see if the title reflects the process as the author sees it.

6. After rereading the selection, mentally note the process and its steps. Also note the author's viewpoint of the process.

Use the reading strategies on page 3 to read the next selection. Then write a line that describes what the process is. Finally, list the steps in the process.

First, prepare a bucket of soapy water and sponge the car. Next, hose off the dirt and wipe the car clean. Wipe the car windows with cleaner and a clean cloth. Finally, vacuum the car interior.

Process:_____

Process Steps:

1._____

2._____

3._____

4._____

5._____

Now try applying this strategy to a longer passage. Read the passage carefully. On the lines that follow, write what process is being described. List some of the descriptive words (descriptors) in the first paragraph that show the author's viewpoint. Then list at least three steps within the process.

Refinishing furniture is a time-consuming activity. Still, the results can be rewarding if each of the following steps is done correctly.

First, choose the desired stain. When choosing the color, consider the wood that you are staining. The same stain will look different on different types of wood. For example, a stain may appear darker on pine than it does on oak.

Next, remove the finish by using a stripper. Spread newspaper around the furniture piece. Then put on gloves and a mask before opening the stripper bottle, as the fumes are toxic. Put about a cup of stripper into an old coffee can. Then begin spreading it on the wood. Wait at least five minutes. Then take an old wallpaper scraper and begin to scrape, moving in the direction of the grain. Dispose of the sludge in another can. Repeat the procedure if necessary. Next, clean the wood. Be sure to follow the manufacturer's directions on the stripper. Once the furniture is dry, use fine steel wool to remove any remaining paint.

Now begin to sand the wood. Use a palm sander with fine sandpaper to remove lingering stain and old varnish. Use a hand sander with extra-fine sandpaper for smaller areas. Continue sanding until the natural wood appears smooth.

After sanding, apply the stain with a clean rag. Stain should be applied with the grain of the wood. Apply the second coat sparingly.

Be sure the stain has dried thoroughly before applying the finish. Brush the polyurethane finish on carefully. Be sure to brush with the grain of the wood in one direction only. Do not apply thickly, or the finish will bubble. After the polyurethane coat has dried, apply a thin second coat. Brush the second polyurethane coat on sparingly.

After the furniture has dried for 24 hours, enjoy!

Process:_____

Descriptors:_____

Steps:_____

The Main Idea

The main idea in the process pattern is the overall process from the author's viewpoint. The author's opinion, or bias, can affect the way the main idea is presented. If the author's bias or attitude toward the process is not stated, the main idea in the process pattern is the process itself.

For example, suppose an author hates camping. That author's description of a camping trip might be very negative. The main idea of the process could be, "Camping is a nightmare." If the author loves camping, the main idea might be, "Camping is a wonderful way to relax." With a neutral author, the main idea might simply be "camping"—in other words, the process itself. Looking for descriptors will help you decide whether or not the author's viewpoint affects the main idea.

Sometimes you can get a clear idea of the author's viewpoint in the first or last paragraph. At other times, you will need to look further. Watch for the author's use of descriptive words. These include adjectives and adverbs, but other word choices can also tell you a lot. Does the process require the reader to *climb* or *scramble*, *carry* or *haul*?

Understanding the author's viewpoint will help you in several ways. If you can tell the author's viewpoint, you can evaluate it for bias. You can use it to identify the main idea of a paragraph. And you can use it when you prepare a title for your outline.

As you read the selection in **Example 4,** note how the author's viewpoint can be found both in the first and last paragraphs, and in the use of descriptors.

Example 4

For many, the smell of toasted marshmallows brings back one of the pleasures of summer campfires. The special tang of burnt sugar unleashes memories. To enjoy this classic treat, you need a fire, marshmallows, a knife, and a stick.

Start by finding a stick that's long enough to keep you a comfortable distance from the fire. Use a knife to sharpen the end to a point. Press a marshmallow firmly onto the pointed end.

Find a reddish-gray coal in the fire. Hold your marshmallow close to the coal. Keep turning it, exposing all sides to the heat.

When it puffs up slightly and is golden brown on all sides, the marshmallow is done. Enjoy!

Descriptors: pleasures, special, enjoy, classic
Viewpoint: positive, happy memories of toasted marshmallows

Read the next selection. Look for the main idea. On the lines that follow, write the name of the process, the descriptors, and the main idea.

Motherhood. America. And that delicious dessert, apple pie. The flaky crust and juicy apples of this favorite treat highlight any meal.

Apple pie is easy to make. First, pick six or seven Granny Smith apples. Peel and slice the apples, and put them in a large bowl. Mix a cup of sugar with a teaspoon of cinnamon. Stir the sugar and cinnamon in with the apples, then set aside.

Put a few ice cubes in a glass with a spoonful or two of water. Set aside. Then mix a cup of shortening with two cups of flour and a teaspoon of salt. Cut the flour and salt into the shortening, using a wire pastry cutter. The mixture is ready when it looks like granules, or tiny dough bits. Now add enough water to dampen the granules. Stir quickly until the granules stick together.

Prepare a pie cloth and rolling pin. Sprinkle some flour on the cloth and on the rolling pin. Next, place half the dough on the cloth and sprinkle it with flour. Use the rolling pin to roll the dough into a circle 2 or 3 inches larger than the pie pan.

Grease the pie pan. Then lift the rolled dough carefully into the pan. Pat the dough into the pan; cut away excess dough around the edges. Put the apple mix into the pan. Sprinkle some pieces of butter on the apples. Set the pan aside.

Roll out the remaining dough. Cut one ¾-inch strip across the widest part of the dough. Carefully lift up the strip and place it over the apples, pressing it into the crust at the edges. Trim the edges. Then cut another strip and place it at right angles to the first strip. Finish criss-crossing dough strips at 1-inch intervals across the top of the pie pan. Bake the pie at 400°F for one hour.

Let the pie cool for two hours. Then cut it into generous wedges. Top each piece with vanilla ice cream. Enjoy this mouthwatering treat!

Process: _____

Descriptors: _____

Main Idea: _____

Titling the Reading: A Guide to the Main Idea

If a reading selection does not have a title, it is helpful to create one. This can help you identify the main idea. It will also help later when you need to give your outline a title. The title should tell what the process is. It also should reflect the author's viewpoint of the process. Try to keep it short—no more than five words.

The passage below describes the steps in processing raisins. Descriptive words suggest that the author feels positively about the process.

Example 5
Clusters of plump grapes hang on the vines. The growers irrigate the grapevines. The grapes grow round and succulent under the hot summer sun. In August, the grape clusters are carefully handpicked. They are placed on rows of clean paper trays near the vines. For the next two or three weeks, the grapes dry in the sun. Then they are placed in wooden bins. The sweet, dried, brown raisins are transported to the processing plant.

At the plant, the raisins are inspected rigorously. Machines take off remaining stems, and the raisins are washed thoroughly. Then they are inspected again, packed in boxes, and shipped to stores all over the world.

The adverbs *carefully*, *rigorously*, and *thoroughly* reflect the author's viewpoint of the process. To show the author's opinion, this outline could be titled "Raisins: Processed With Care."

Titling Strategies

Sometimes it is easy to think of a title for a reading passage. At other times, you may need to use a system. If you cannot think of a title, try to "build" one by following these steps:

1. Use words like *actions, procedure, process,* or *steps* in your title.

2. Add a descriptive word that shows the author's view of the process.

3. Include a word that names the process.

4. Limit your title to five words.

Read the next selection to identify the process. Look for descriptors that show the author's viewpoint or bias about the process. Then title the selection. Write the name of the process, key descriptors, and your title on the lines below the reading.

Baseball making is a complex, precise process. The baseball begins as a pill—a small sphere of cork and rubber encased in a rubber shell. The standard pill weighs 0.85 ounces and is 1.375 inches in diameter.

Then the pill is lightly wound with three different layers of wool yarn. The yarn itself, with its twists and kinks, is important. It determines the weight of the ball. New (not recycled) wool, with no synthetic fibers, makes the best yarn. Processed wool and acrylics are also used to produce a less expensive ball. In winding the yarn, tension is crucial. If the yarn has too much tension or is too flat, it takes more yarn to form a ball of the correct size. This excess yarn makes the ball too heavy. A lively ball, with an acceptable size and weight, is made by winding the yarn tightly at first, then decreasing the tension as the winding continues.

Once the yarns have been wound to form a core, a small layer of cotton/polyester finishing yarn is added. The finishing yarn keeps the ball yarn tight and holds the ball together.

The ball is then dipped in latex cement so that the cover will stick to the ball core. The tacky latex surface also makes the sewing process easier.

Cover materials are typically made of alum-tanned leather. This material is the best leather for sewing and for long life. Covers made of split leather and synthetics are also used to produce a cheaper baseball.

The final step is sewing the cover to the ball. This involves cutting the leather, sewing and flattening the seams, and sewing 108 red-cotton stitches on the cover. Then the finished ball is stamped, packaged, and shipped around the country. The white and red-trimmed orb finally winds its way out of the pitcher's mitt into the batter's zone. Let's play ball!

Process: _____

Descriptors: _____

Title: _____

Renaming Substeps

The process pattern in longer readings is usually made up of steps (major actions) and substeps (minor actions). Sometimes the substeps can be confusing. You need to distinguish between major steps in the process and substeps, which make up the major steps. In short readings, the major steps are usually clearly stated. However, in longer ones, you may have to combine and rename several substeps to make one major step. Of course, you will still need to keep track of the substeps in each major step. These will be the supporting details in your outline.

The example below describes the first steps in jump-starting a car. Some of the major steps actually consist of several substeps. These can also be called "minor details." You do not need to remember each substep to understand the whole process. However, you do need to understand all the major steps (also called "primary details"). Thus, major steps are the building blocks of the process design. Major steps may be recalled or restated by the reader.

In the selection below, the reader must note the major steps in order to understand how cars are jump-started. Notice how substeps are combined and renamed to identify major steps.

Example 6

Forgetting to switch off a car's headlights can drain the battery. To start the car, you will need a jump-start. This requires help, as you will need a car with a good battery to jump-start the dead one. Make sure both car batteries have the same voltage; check the user's manuals if you don't know the car voltages.

Park the "good-battery" car so that the car batteries are close to each other. However, the cars themselves should not touch. Engage the emergency brakes on both cars. Finally, turn off electrical systems in the car with the dead battery.

> **Major Step (Primary Detail):** prepare both vehicles for jump-starting the dead car
> **Substeps (Minor Details):** locate a working car; check that voltages match; check manuals if needed; park car; set brakes; turn off electrical systems

Get out the jumper cables. Usually the positive cable is red and the negative cable is black. Before connecting the jumper cables, know the location of the positive and negative battery terminals. Consult the owner's manual for specific directions. Failure to follow specific directions may cause bodily injury and damage to the car's charging system.

> **Major Step (Primary Detail):** prepare to connect jumper cables
> **Substeps (Minor Details):** locate cables; identify positive and negative cables; consult manual if needed

Word Clues

Ordering words such as *first, second, third, next, also,* and *finally* can help you recognize major steps within the process pattern. Action verbs that label major steps and substeps can give additional clues. Words like *action, process, procedure(s)*, and *steps(s)* indicate the process pattern. They also denote major steps in the overall process.

Here are the remaining steps in the jump-starting process. Each major step includes ordering words. Read the passage below carefully. Note each major step and its word clues.

Example 7

Remove metal jewelry, especially rings. While connecting the jumper cables to the car batteries, be careful that the red and black clamps on each end of the jumper cables do not touch each other. Then, unless the owner's manual states otherwise, connect a red clamp to the terminal post of the bad battery labeled positive (+). Connect the other red clamp on the opposite end of the jumper cable to the terminal post of the good battery labeled positive (+). Connect one black clamp to the terminal post of the good battery labeled negative (−). Finally, connect the black clamp on the opposite end of the jumper cable to any grounded part on the engine block of the bad-battery car. While connecting the jumper cables, avoid touching moving parts, such as belts or fan blades, or any other metal.

> **Major Step (Primary Detail):** connect the jumper cables
> **Substeps (Minor Details):** remove jewelry; avoid contact between red and black clamps; connect red clamps to positive terminals; connect black clamp to negative terminal; connect other black clamp to engine block; avoid touching moving parts or metal
> **Word Clues:** *then, finally, connect*

Next, turn on the ignition of the bad-battery car. If the dead battery does not start right away, start the motor on the good-battery car for a few seconds. Then try starting the other car again. If the dead-battery car still does not start, check the cable connection. Wait a few minutes, and then try again.

> **Major Step (Primary Detail):** start the dead-battery car
> **Substeps (Minor Details):** try to start car; troubleshoot if car does not start
> **Word Clues:** *next, turn on, start, try, check, wait, try*

Read the following passages to find the process. Note the major steps and substeps in each paragraph. Underline the word clues in each paragraph. Then rename each major step (primary detail) as broadly as possible. Fill in the substeps. Finally, name the process as a whole.

To keep a vehicle in good operating shape, you should change the oil every 3,000 miles or every three months. To do so, you will need new oil recommended for your vehicle and a good-quality oil filter.

To begin, park the car on a level surface and apply the parking brake. Then run the engine until it reaches operating temperature. Turn the engine off. Unscrew the oil cap on the top of the engine to allow for a better flow of oil. Crawl under the car and look for the oil tank—a large tank with a protruding bolt. Some lower-lying cars may require jacking up the front end of the vehicle so you can crawl underneath. Two jack stands on either side of the car will ensure that the car stays safely secured. Place a large, shallow pan under the bolt of the oil tank. Then remove the bolt or sump plug with a wrench. Let the oil drain into the pan.

Major Step (Primary Detail): _____

Substeps: _____

In the meantime, locate the oil filter on the side of the engine. Put the filter wrench around the filter. Gently rotate in a counterclockwise direction. Remove the filter. Wipe the filter-mounting surface with a clean rag. Coat the rubber gasket on the new filter with clean engine oil. Then screw in the new filter by rotating it in a clockwise direction. Do not over-tighten. Once the filter makes contact with the engine, tighten with an additional three-quarter turn.

Major Step (Primary Detail): _____

Substeps: _____

Pour the new oil into the engine. Check the owner's manual for the proper amount (usually four to five quarts). Then check the dipstick to see if the proper amount has been added. Check under the car for leaks before starting the engine. Dispose of the old oil properly.

Major Step (Primary Detail): _____

Substeps: _____

Process: _____

Using a Graphic Organizer

You can use a graphic organizer like the one that follows to prepare for making the outline. In the central circle, write the name of the process. Write the first major step in the appropriate segment of the innermost ring. Write the substeps (minor details) in the other segments of that ring. Add the next major steps and substeps to the next ring, and so on. Add rings to the organizer as necessary. The completed organizer should give you a clear overview of the process.

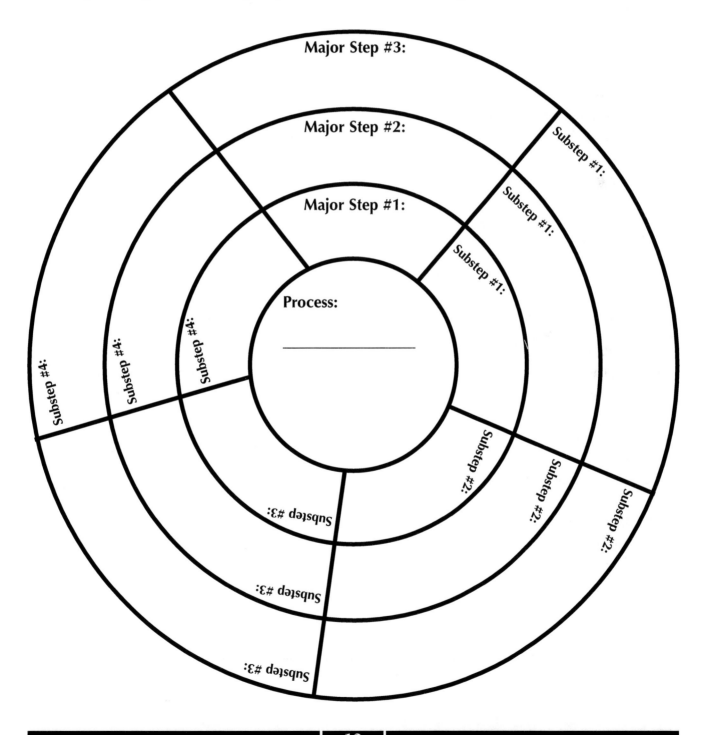

Designing the Process Pattern Outline

In a process pattern outline, each major step of the process has a Roman-numeral heading. Each substep is a capital-letter entry. As always, the outline moves from general to specific as the entries move from left to right. You will recall that **Example 3** discusses how to drive safely. Here is what an outline based on that example might look like:

Driving a Car Safely
    I. Fasten seat belts
    II. Adjust mirrors
        A. Turn left mirror
        B. Turn right mirror
        C. Adjust rearview mirror
    III. Turn on the ignition
    IV. Move from driveway to street
        A. Check for pedestrians before shifting
        B. Reverse slowly down driveway
        C. Turn into street and shift gears
        D. Drive carefully down street

Building a Process Outline

Building a process outline involves combining the steps you have learned about in this chapter. You may want to use the graphic organizer as you collect the information you need for each heading. When the organizer is completed, use it to fill in your outline.

1. Read the selection carefully. Note the major steps in the process.

2. List at least two major steps. Enter them in sequence as Roman-numeral headings.

3. List at least two substeps under each Roman-numeral heading. Give them capital-letter entries.

4. List supporting details related to each substep. Give them Arabic-numeral entries.

5. Finally, title the outline. Try to capture the process and the author's viewpoint.

Read the following passage. Then, on the next page, build a short outline for the reading by using the steps described on page 14. Do not use more than four Roman-numeral headings.

The most important item needed for this project is the plaster bandage. It is commonly used to form a cast for broken bones. The bandage comes as a 3- or 4-inch roll of gauze filled with dried plaster. You can buy it at a medical supply house or at most art stores. Each plaster-gauze roll makes 2½ face masks.

Protect the work surface with newspapers. Cut the bandage into strips of varying lengths, from a few inches to 9 or 10 inches. The longest strips should reach from the subject's forehead to the chin, with room for the nose.

Next, spread a generous amount of petroleum jelly over the subject's face. This will keep the plaster from sticking to the face. Take care to cover the eyelids, lips, and eyebrows.

Dip the strips into a bowl of water, squeezing out excess water. Start applying strips in horizontal layers, from one side of the face to the other. Smooth each strip carefully as it is applied. Then overlap in vertical layers. Fill in and thicken facial areas with layered strips. Reinforce the nose and cheek areas with smaller strips.

After about 30–40 minutes, the mask will be dry enough to remove. Before you take it off, examine the mask to see if any area needs additional reinforcement. If so, add more strips where needed. Wait another 30 minutes for the added strips to dry. If not, pull the mask off gently. Starting at the chin, use your thumbs to pry the mask up. Then let the mask dry untouched for 24 hours.

After the mask is thoroughly dry, decorate it. If a natural plaster color is desired, seal it with a clear acrylic sealer. Otherwise, paint it with acrylic paints. Then glue on feathers, sequins, and glitter as desired.

Outline Title: _____

  I. _____

     A. _____

     B. _____

  II. _____

     A. _____

     B. _____

     C. _____

  III. _____

     A. _____

     B. _____

     C. _____

  IV. _____

     A. _____

     B. _____

Here is a longer reading selection to practice on. Follow the same steps as you did in Activity 6, but create your own outline on a separate sheet of paper. Use no more than three Roman-numeral headings. Note: Proper outline style means that you should not have just one capital-letter entry; you must have at least two.

The first step in building a compost pile is planning its location. First, the pile should not be located near a structure or building. Second, the pile must be close to water, but located away from traffic. Third, the pile should be near a wall or tree to prevent the wind from drying the compost. The pile should be distant from pine trees and vegetable gardens. This will prevent pine needles and garden insects from slowing down the decomposition process. Finally, the pile must be easy to access for adding, removing, and stirring.

The next step is to determine the size. For proper aeration, the compost pile should be at least 1 cubic yard, but no larger than 5 square feet at 4 to 5 feet high. Depending on size, the bin may be made with railroad ties or bricks.

After planning, the compost pile can be constructed. First, soak the ground underneath the pile. Then dig a trench across the center of the base. Cover the trench with a stiff hardware cloth. To build the pile, put down a 4- to 6-inch layer of coarse carbon twigs and wood chips. If a shredder is available, shred or chop organic materials before depositing them on the pile. Add a 1- to 2-inch layer of nitrogenous material (like manure) sprinkled with fertilizer. Then add a layer of soil or sod about an inch thick. Continue layering with chopped or shredded organic material—leaves, grass clippings, weeds, chopped corncobs, stalks, and/or sawdust. Alternate with nitrogenous layers of manure and fertilizer. Do not add diseased plants to the compost pile. Do not add weeds that have gone to seed.

Water between layers. Do not layer material more than 4–6 inches deep. After firming each layer of organic material, add an occasional shovelful of soil to keep the compost in place. When the bin is nearly full, make a final layer of carbon materials. Add water to this layer.

After the compost pile is finished, let it sit for several days before turning the compost. But be careful. If the pile has been well constructed, its moisture content may be 50 percent water. Its temperature may be over 140° Fahrenheit. When the temperature of the pile decreases, turn the compost by lifting all of the outside material to the middle of the compost pile. As the materials decompose during the next several weeks, the pile will shrink to one half its original height and to 70 to 80 percent of its original volume. After the compost has decomposed, it becomes a powdery, dark-brown material called humus. Humus is used as a mulching material in gardening and in landscaping.

Recognizing the Pattern

The **problem/solution** pattern is an easy one to spot. Once you spot the problem in a reading passage, the solution is usually not hard to find. You can find this two-part pattern in articles that discuss issues and how to improve or fix them. In school, the problem/solution pattern is often found in science textbooks. It also appears in readings about psychology, social studies, technology, driver's education, and other subjects.

In the problem/solution pattern, the problem is presented first. It is then followed by a solution. The solution may be presented in a series of steps, or it may be a list of possible choices. Here are some simple examples of the problem/solution pattern.

Example 1 (Solution in a series of steps)

Problem: Sue was employed at Hamburger Heaven on the evening shift. She worked closely with Bob, the night manager. After a few weeks, Bob asked Sue out after work. Sue didn't know how to respond. She didn't think a dating relationship at work was a good idea. Unknown to Bob, she had a steady boyfriend, Jim. Sue was somewhat attracted to Bob. She thought about breaking up with Jim. What should she do?

Solution: After thinking about her problem, Sue told Bob that she wasn't interested in dating him. She then told Jim that she wanted to end their relationship. Now Sue is free to date other guys.

Example 2 (Solution as a list of possible choices)

Problem: Sue was employed at Hamburger Heaven on the evening shift. She worked closely with Bob, the night manager. After a few weeks, Bob asked Sue out after work. Sue didn't know how to respond because she had a steady boyfriend, Jim. She also didn't think a dating relationship at work was a good idea.

Solution: Sue had several choices. She could go out with Bob and lie to Jim. She could break up with Jim and go out with Bob. Or she could break up with Jim and refuse to date Bob. She chose the third action.

Characteristics of the Problem/Solution Pattern

The problem/solution pattern often includes nouns and verbs such as *problem, issue, dilemma, solution, alternative, choice, solve,* or *resolve.* Look at **Example 1.** Notice that the word *problem* in the second paragraph refers to the information in the first paragraph. The word *problem* also tells the reader that a solution may follow. Now look at **Example 2.** What important word in the solution tells the reader about possible ways to solve the problem?

Like the process pattern, the problem/solution pattern uses active verbs to show major steps within the problem and its solution. In **Example 1,** these active verbs include *worked, asked,* and *told.*

Major steps (or solution choices) may be introduced by ordering words like *first, second, next,* or *finally.* Look at **Examples 1** and **2** again. There are no ordering words in either example. When do you think ordering words are necessary?

If a reading passage contains an issue or challenge along with one or more ways in which the challenge can be resolved, it is probably an example of the problem/solution pattern.

The paragraph in **Example 3** describes a familiar problem/solution. We recognize this pattern because of the word *problem* in the first line. The paragraph is followed by a line that names the problem. Then the solution and solution steps are listed.

> **Example 3**
> Mother had a problem with Marie's room. She informed Marie that she could not go to the dance unless she changed her sloppy housekeeping habits. Mother told Marie that she had to start making her bed, hanging up her clothes, dumping her trash, and organizing her drawers.
>
> > **Problem:** Mother was unhappy with Marie's room.
> > **Solution:** getting Marie to change her housekeeping habits
> > **Solution Steps:** making bed, hanging up clothes, dumping trash, and organizing drawers

Problem/Solution Pattern

Once you identify a problem/solution pattern in your reading, these strategies can help you read and understand the material:

1. Read the first paragraph carefully. Try to figure out the problem. Skim the rest of the selection to figure out if there is more than one solution.

2. Read the last paragraph carefully. See how the problem is solved. Look for words such as *solution, resolution, fix, improve,* and *remedy* as you read.

3. Read the whole selection. Look for action verbs that show major steps within both problem and solution. Look for ordering words like *first, second,* or *finally.* These words may show the order of major steps in the solution (or solution choices).

4. If many solutions are listed, look for words like *alternative, another,* or *choice.* Then look to see if there is a best choice.

5. Reread the selection. This time, look for adjectives and adverbs that may indicate the author's opinion. Often the first and last paragraphs present the author's view of the problem and its solution.

6. Figure out if the author's opinion is the main idea behind the problem and solution. See if the same opinion is captured in the title. Look for descriptive words (adjectives or adverbs) in the title that reflect the author's viewpoint.

7. Review the problem and the solution. Then review the main idea, the author's viewpoint of the problem/solution, and the major steps involved.

Read the next selection. Use the strategies described on page 20 as you read. Then state the problem in the space provided. Also list the solution and the solution steps on the next two lines.

Yesterday I wore my best dress pants to school for picture day. Things were fine until after English, when I noticed a big, blue stain on my front pocket. I didn't want to tell Mom, so my solution was to wash the pants myself.

I found some directions on a can of dry-cleaning fluid and followed them step by step. First, I forced water through the stain to remove excess ink. Then I applied the dry-cleaning fluid. Next, I soaked the stain in warm water with three tablespoons of household ammonia. Finally, I washed my pants in the washing machine. Miraculously, the stain disappeared.

Problem: _____

Solution: _____

Solution Steps: 1. _____

2. _____

3. _____

4. _____

Now try this approach with a longer selection. Using problem/solution reading strategies, read the next passage. On the lines that follow, write the problem that is being described. List the descriptive word (descriptor) in the first paragraph that shows the author's viewpoint. Then list at least three steps within the solution.

Dear Tom,

A couple of months ago, I bought a new car. My dad is telling me to take it to the garage to have it checked over before winter comes. I'm a responsible driver. I know I have to put antifreeze in so the motor won't blow up. Does the car really need anything else? I don't have a lot of money.

Thanks,
Mike

Dear Mike,

You should have your car checked over every autumn. The winter months can cause a lot of wear and tear on vehicles. As you mentioned, adding antifreeze to your radiator is very important. Antifreeze prevents the water in the car motor from freezing. If the water should freeze, your motor might blow, or your radiator could crack.

A car checkup should also include inspecting the battery. Battery failure is common in cold weather. The cables and the battery charge should also be checked. And the windshield wipers, distributor cap, points, spark plugs, and spark-plug cables should be looked over. Hoses and belts should be inspected and replaced if necessary.

Review your car manual. Know the recommended air pressure for your tires. Have your tires inspected, too. Replace cracked, bubbled, or bald tires. Driving on defective tires is dangerous. Also, replace tires with worn treads. A tread is worn if the top of Lincoln's head shows when you insert an overturned penny into the shallow tread groove.

Finally, after your car has been checked, do your best to maintain it during the winter!

Good luck,
Tom

Problem: _____

Descriptor(s): _____

Solution Steps: _____

_____

The Main Idea

The main idea in the problem/solution pattern is the central statement, or theme, behind the problem and its solution. For example, the reading about Marie's messy room could be written to show the central idea that many teenagers do not like to pick up after themselves. In this way, many problem/solution readings can serve as examples for central ideas.

The problem and solution are presented according to the author's viewpoint. Thus, the author's bias can show. For example, from the descriptor *sloppy*, you can guess that the author probably agrees with Marie's mother about Marie's room.

You can sometimes find a clear idea of the author's viewpoint in the first or last paragraph. At other times, you will need to look at the author's use of descriptive words. These include adjectives and adverbs, but other word choices can also tell you a lot. Does the author state why the problem occurred? Does the author recommend certain actions to solve the problem?

Understanding the author's viewpoint will help you in several ways. If you can figure out the author's opinion, you can weigh it for bias. You can use it to identify the main idea of a paragraph. And you can use it when you prepare a title for your outline.

Read the selection in **Example 4.** Note how the author's viewpoint can be found in the first paragraph. Look for the use of descriptors.

Example 4

Driving on slippery, icy roads is dangerous. Many drivers fail to change their driving habits for hazardous road conditions. Therefore, accidents and injuries can occur.

To drive safely, the driver first should prepare for poor weather conditions by clearing and defrosting car windows. Also, the driver should keep a full tank of gas in the winter. A high level of gas prevents water from condensing in the gas tank.

When out on slippery roads, the driver should slow down. This is because slick roads require more distance for the driver to slow down, or decelerate. A car should be at least three car distances away from any other vehicle. If the car should skid, the brakes should *not* be applied. Instead, the driver should remove his or her foot from the gas pedal. The driver should then decelerate slowly and steer gently. When the car straightens, it will regain its traction and control. Finally, every passenger should wear a seat belt.

Descriptors: *slippery, dangerous, hazardous*
Viewpoint: Driving on hazardous roads requires special safety rules.

23

Read the next selection. Look for the main idea. On the lines that follow, write the name of the process. Also write the descriptors and the main idea.

Several hundred years ago, the peregrine falcon was commonly seen in the Midwest. A graceful bird, the peregrine falcon was noted for its beauty and speed. However, by the late 1800s, the peregrine falcon fell prey to nest robbing and random destruction. It was on the verge of extinction.

To save the peregrine falcon, the World Bird Sanctuary launched a restoration project in 1985. The project was based in St. Louis, Missouri. The goal was to help increase the number of peregrine falcons in the Midwest. This involved raising and releasing young falcons in several cities. In 1992, the Missouri Department of Conservation released 24 young peregrine falcons in downtown Kansas City. Peregrine falcons from Kansas City were later spotted in Des Moines, Iowa, and in Omaha, Nebraska.

The restoration project was successful. Peregrine falcons have since been reclassified as a threatened, not an endangered, species.

Process: _____

Descriptors: _____

Main Idea: _____

Titling the Reading: A Guide to the Main Idea

If a reading selection does not have a title, it is helpful to create one. This can help you identify the main idea. It will also help later when you need to give your outline a title. The title should tell what the problem/solution is. It should also reflect the author's viewpoint. Try to keep the title short—no more than five words. The selection below describes a common teenage problem. Descriptive words tell how unhappy the author is about the situation.

Example 5

Dear Editor:

I am a senior in high school. I have a brother two years younger than me. My parents bought a new car a couple of months ago. My mom said I could drive her old station wagon. That has worked out fine, since my brother only has his driving permit.

Next month, my brother turns 16. Then he'll get his license. He says he'll be able to use the station wagon. Mom says I have to share it with him.

I think she's mean. I had to wait two years before I got a car to use. Before that, I had to share Mom's car. Now she says I have to share the station wagon.

Next fall I'm going away to college. My brother will keep the car then. He'll get to drive it all by himself and won't have to share with me. I think this is unfair, and I'm mad.

Thanks,
Anna

Dear Anna:

Your brother is getting a better deal. Talk it over with your Mom. She'll probably work something out. Maybe she'll let you drive her new car—sometimes.

The adjectives *mean, unfair,* and *mad* plainly show the author's opinion about having to share cars with her younger brother. A title such as "An Unfair Deal" would reflect the author's viewpoint.

Titling Strategies

Sometimes it is easy to think of a title for a reading. At other times, you may need to use a system. If you cannot think of a good title, try to "build" one by following these steps:

1. Use words like *options, problem, solution, solving, tips, alternative,* or *alternate* in your title.

2. Add nouns or adjectives that show the author's view of the problem and/or the solution.

3. Limit your title to five words.

Read the passage below. Identify the problem/solution. While you read, look for descriptors that show the author's viewpoint or bias regarding the process. Then title your selection. Write the problem/solution, key descriptors, and your title on the lines below the reading.

Unhealthy hair may reflect the saying, "You are what you eat." Dry, brittle hair may point to an unhealthy diet. Improper hair-care habits can compound hair damage. This leads to an unattractive hair look.

Revitalizing your hair is not difficult. However, this solution may take time. First, examine your diet. Eliminate fried foods that are high in saturated fats. Cut back on carbohydrates. Instead, eat foods high in protein. Protein intake is necessary for healthy hair growth.

Next, check out your hair-care habits. A healthy scalp is a must for beautiful hair. Add 20 crushed aspirin tablets to your shampoo bottle. Gently massage your scalp with this mix as you wash your hair. It will increase the scalp's blood circulation and promote hair growth. If conditioners are necessary, apply them at the ends of your hair. Do not use mousse or styling gels. Don't use harsh conditioners or shampoos. They will cause flaky buildup on your scalp. Rather, opt for vitamin-enriched hair products that make your hair livelier.

Finally, if at all possible, avoid hot hair dryers. Dryers cause heat damage to your hair. Let your hair dry naturally. You can also hand-dry your hair to increase scalp circulation.

After a few months, your good hair-care habits should pay off. Your beautiful new-hair look will be your treasure!

Problem/Solution: _____

Descriptors: _____

Title: _____

Renaming Substeps

The problem/solution pattern in longer readings usually contains steps (major actions) and substeps (minor actions). Both the problem and the solution may include steps and substeps. Sometimes the substeps can be confusing. You need to distinguish between the major steps in the problem/solution and substeps that make up the major steps.

In short readings, the major steps are usually clearly stated. Sometimes, alternate solutions also are introduced as major steps. Each alternate solution, or solution choice, is a major step. These solutions, as major steps, can include substeps.

The passage below gives a list of possible ways to treat shinsplints. Each solution choice (major step) consists of one or more substeps (minor actions, or minor details). You do not need to remember all the substeps to understand the solution. Each alternative is a major step (also called a primary detail). Major steps should be recalled by the reader.

Example 6

In the spring, many runners make up for their lack of winter activity with great bursts of exercise. They run too much, too soon. Many runners develop muscle fatigue from too little muscle tone. When combined with tough workouts on rough, uneven surfaces, poor tone may lead to shinsplints. Shinsplints are tiny tears in the muscles attached to the shin. Shinsplints cause runners much pain.

Ice is one way to promote healing. It reduces swelling. The injured runner should place ice on the painful area, both before and after exercise, for 10 to 15 minutes. The runner may also take anti-inflammatories along with the ice treatment. One example is ibuprofen. Along with ice, it can ease lower-leg pain.

> **Major Step (Primary Detail):** Apply ice on affected area.
> **Substeps (Minor Details):** Use ice before and after exercising; ice for 10 to 15 minutes; take ibuprofen.

Stretching and massaging the shin area are vital in helping to heal the inflamed muscles. Taping the shins after massaging them may help to lessen the pain during healing.

> **Major Step (Primary Detail):** stretching and massaging shin area
> **Substep (Minor Detail):** taping shins after massaging

However, the best way to heal lower-leg muscle tears is to limit leg movement. If runners feel shooting pains up the insides of their calves, they should stop running. If walking is painful, runners should also stop walking. Shinsplint treatment requires time away from exercise. Rest allows muscle tears to heal.

> **Major Step (Primary Detail):** Limit leg movement.
> **Substeps (Minor Details):** Runners should not feel shooting pain up insides of calves; walkers should not feel pain when walking.

Unlike short passages, longer problem/solution readings may be more difficult. You may need to combine substeps and rename several substeps as one major step. You should still try to keep track of the substeps within each major step. These substeps will be the supporting details in your outline.

The next example tells how to avoid the problem of poor table manners. Some of the major steps within the solution actually include substeps (minor details). You do not need to remember all these substeps to understand the solution. However, you do need to understand all the major steps (primary details). Major steps are the building blocks of the problem/solution design. Major steps should be recalled by the reader.

In the selection below, note each major step to understand how to avoid poor table manners. Notice how the substeps are combined and renamed to identify major steps.

Example 7
Jim's first formal dinner is not a comfortable experience. Upon sitting down, he looks at the table and notices unfamiliar settings. He isn't sure how to act.

Although Jim does not realize it, the solution to his dining problem is nearby. It lies both in his common sense and in his power of observation. First, Jim must act as directed by his hostess. When he first sits down, he should place his napkin on his lap. If the guests are asked to begin eating, he may eat. If not, he should wait until all the guests are served and his hostess starts to eat.

> **Major Step (Primary Detail):** follow directions of hostess
> **Substeps (Minor Details):** place napkin in lap; wait until all guests are served and hostess begins eating

Then, Jim should watch to see how the other guests sit. He must sit straight with his arms near his body. He should not lean back in his seat or forward with his elbows on the table.

> **Major Step (Primary Detail):** keep proper dining posture
> **Substeps (Minor Details):** sit straight with arms near body; do not lean back in chair; do not lean forward with elbows on the table

Word Clues

Ordering words such as *first, second, third, next, also,* and *finally* can help you recognize major steps or solution choices. Action verbs that label major steps and substeps can give more clues. Words such as *problem, solution, alternatives, choices, solved,* and *resolved* indicate the problem/solution pattern. They often introduce major steps or alternate solutions within the pattern.

Here are the remaining steps in observing good table manners. Each major step is introduced by ordering words. Read the selection carefully. Note each major step and its word clues.

Example 8

Next, Jim must use his table utensils properly. For multicourse meals, he should remember to use his utensils from the outside in. Once Jim uses a utensil, he should not place it on the table again. He should not prop it against a plate. Instead, he should lay it across the plate. Jim should use the butter knife to place butter on his butter plate. When he uses a soup spoon, he should not fill the spoon completely with soup. Jim should not bang the spoon into the bottom of his soup bowl when eating. Above all, he must not slurp his soup.

> **Major Step (Primary Detail):** Use table utensils correctly.
> **Substeps (Minor Details):** use table utensils from outside in; lay used utensil across the plate; use butter knife to place butter on plate; eat soup neatly and quietly
> **Word Clues:** *next*

Also, Jim should observe general table manners. He should pass items promptly when asked to the person next to him. He should not pass things across the table. Jim must not talk with his mouth full. He must chew with his mouth shut. He should never grab food.

> **Major Step (Primary Detail):** Observe general table manners.
> **Substeps (Minor Details):** pass items promptly to person next to him; do not talk with a full mouth; chew with mouth shut; do not grab food
> **Word Clues:** *also*

Finally, after Jim has finished eating, he should lay his knife and fork diagonally across his plate. They should extend from the bottom right to the top left of his plate. When everyone has finished eating and drinking, he should place his napkin next to his plate. Then, after thanking his hostess, Jim may leave the table.

> **Major Step (Primary Detail):** Use after-dinner manners.
> **Substeps (Minor Details):** lay knife and fork diagonally across plate; place napkin next to plate; thank hostess
> **Word Clues:** *finally, finished*

Read the following passage. Find the problem and solution. Underline the word clues in each paragraph. Then rename each major step as broadly as possible. Fill in the substeps. Finally, name the problem and solution as a whole.

Accidental home shootings often occur among children. They result in injuries and sometimes death. Law enforcement and educational agencies try to reduce these accidents. However, the final responsibility to keep the home environment safe rests with parents.

The most important step in preventing gun violence is to keep guns away from children. Avoid storing guns in the home. However, if a gun is kept, it should be unloaded and secured in a locked location. Ammunition should be stored safely in another locked location, away from the gun. Keys to both secured locations should be kept away from children.

Major Step (Primary Detail): _____

Substeps:_____

Parents who own guns must teach their children about the dangers of firearms. Children should be taught not to touch or handle guns. They also should be told to seek help from a parent or trusted adult if they find a gun anywhere in the home or elsewhere.

Major Step (Primary Detail): _____

Substeps:_____

Finally, parents must talk to their children about the dangers of misusing guns to express emotions. They should point out how often this is shown in the media. Parents must explain that media violence is not a positive model for real-life situations. Parents also must stress that healthy ways to resolve conflict do not include the use of guns. Children need to know the effects of gun violence: death or injury.

Major Step (Primary Detail): _____

Substeps:_____

Problem: _____

Solution: _____

Using a Graphic Organizer

A graphic organizer like the one that follows can help you prepare for making an outline. First, identify the problem described in the reading. Write it in the space shown at the top of the organizer. Do the same for the solution in the middle of the organizer. Write the first major step for the problem in the space marked. Write the substeps (minor details) briefly under the first major step. Do the same thing for the remaining major steps. Then fill out the solution steps in the same manner as the problem steps. If there are alternatives within the solution, fill in each alternative as a major step. Write the substeps underneath. The completed organizer should give you a clear overview of the problem/solution.

Problem:

Major Step #1:	**Major Step #3:**
Substeps #1:	**Substeps #3:**
Major Step #2:	**Major Step #4:**
Substeps #2:	**Substeps #4:**

Solution:

Major Step #1: **(Alternative #1):**	**Major Step #3:** **(Alternative #3):**
Substeps #1:	**Substeps #3:**
Major Step #2: **(Alternative #2):**	**Major Step #4:** **(Alternative #4):**
Substeps #2:	**Substeps #4:**

Designing the Problem/Solution Pattern Outline

In a problem/solution outline, give the problem the first Roman-numeral heading. Give the solution the second Roman-numeral heading. Each major step within the problem or solution is a capital-letter entry. Alternate solutions also may be listed as capital-letter entries under the solution heading. Next, each substep is listed as an Arabic-numeral entry. It goes under its capital-letter entry (major step). As always, the outline moves from general to specific as the entries move from left to right. You will recall that **Example 4** discussed how to drive on slippery roads. Here is what an outline based on that example might look like:

Driving Safely on Slippery Roads
  I. Danger of slippery roads
  II. Need for new driving habits
    A. Clear and defrost car windows
    B. Maintain full tank of gas
    C. Slow down
    D. Do not brake in skid
      1. Remove foot from gas pedal
      2. Decelerate slowly
      3. Steer in desired direction
    E. Wear a seat belt

Building a Problem/Solution Outline

To build a problem/solution outline, you must combine the steps you have learned in the chapter. You can use the graphic organizer on page 31 to prepare for your outline. It will help you organize the information you need for each heading. When the organizer is completed, use it to fill in your outline.

1. Determine the problem and the solution. Write the problem down as Roman-numeral one. Write the solution down as Roman-numeral two.

2. Note the major steps within the problem and solution. If there is more than one possible solution, list these as capital-letter entries.

3. If there are substeps, list at least two under the appropriate capital-letter entry. Substeps are Arabic-numeral entries.

4. Finally, title the outline. Try to capture the problem/solution and the author's viewpoint in very few words.

32

Following the steps listed on page 32, make a short outline for the next passage. Do not use more than two Roman-numeral headings.

Do you have a problem throwing away old papers, programs, and other "souvenirs"? If so, you may have a clutter problem. Your room is probably disorganized and uncomfortable. You may have very little living space. Perhaps you cannot find specific items amid the chaos. You spend too much time trying to locate the things you need.

Ease your frustration. Give up living in a world of junk by reducing the clutter.

First, use it or lose it. Toss out things that are not used regularly. Do not save any items for future use. Most likely they will simply be misplaced or lost.

Next, find a place for everything. Store items close to where they are used. Put needed articles, such as your cell phone and your keys, in logical places.

Then be sure to pick up after yourself. Return objects to the same location after using them. Be consistent about putting your stuff away. If you fail to place valued articles in special places, you will not be able to find them again.

Finally, give away things that you no longer want. Give unworn clothes and shoes to someone who needs them. Clean out your closets regularly.

Reducing home clutter creates a restful room environment. This provides a sense of well-being. Good management skills at home help build a positive self-image.

Outline Title: _____

   I. _____

      A. _____

      B. _____

  II. _____

      A. _____

      B. _____

      C. _____

        1. _____

        2. _____

Here is a longer reading selection. Follow the same steps as you did in Activity 13. This time, though, create your own outline on a separate sheet of paper. Use no more than two Roman-numeral headings. Remember, proper outline style means that you should not have just one capital-letter entry under a heading. You must have at least two. If you have Arabic-numeral headings, there should be at least two of those as well.

Have you ever met someone who looks familiar but whom you could not place? Memory lapses are common. Sometimes they are unavoidable. No one can remember everything. However, having good habits may increase your mental capacity.

Getting enough sleep refreshes the brain. A tired brain cannot think well. Sleeping for at least eight hours per night renews the brain's ability to recall information.

Eating well is also important. Avoiding caffeine and carbonated drinks can increase your thinking abilities. Cutting down on refined carbohydrates can reduce the drastic ups and downs in blood-sugar levels. Eating high-protein food instead causes an even, sustained blood-sugar level. Nuts, cheese, and eggs are good protein choices.

Multivitamins and mineral supplements may also help boost your mental power. Vitamin B_{12} is especially healthful.

Physical exercise stimulates the brain. Even moderate exercise such as walking works well. It increases blood flow, which is helpful to the heart and circulatory system. Exercise "clears the brain" by diverting blood flow from the brain to the rest of the body. Psychologically, exercise creates a feeling of well-being. This promotes good mental health.

Mental exercise also keeps the brain sharp and active. Reading, playing the piano, and playing thinking games like chess and checkers are good activities.

Finally, understanding how the brain works is vital. People have different learning styles. Most are visual learners; they recall what they see. They benefit from writing things down. Making memory notebooks and signs also helps them. Others are auditory learners. They remember what they hear. They may benefit from listening to tapes or recordings. Still other people are kinesthetic learners. They remember what they do. They can recall information that they have keyboarded, written down, or even modeled.

Activities that support the mind are healthy. Since a healthy mind is a wonderful gift, you should do your best to keep yours in shape.

Recognizing the Pattern

The **cause/effect** pattern is easy to identify. Once you spot the cause in a reading, the effect is sure to follow. You can find this two-part pattern in articles discussing the results of certain actions or events. In school, the cause/effect pattern is often found in science textbooks. It also appears in readings for social studies, psychology, technology, driver's education, and other classes.

In the cause/effect pattern, one or more causes are first presented. They are followed by one or more effects. Both cause(s) and effect(s) may be presented in a series of steps. Or they may be presented in list form. Here are some simple examples of the cause/effect pattern.

Example 1
Cause/effect in sequential steps

Cause: Yesterday was Keisha's bad day. First, she had forgotten to set her alarm clock and overslept by two hours. Next, she realized that her gas tank was empty, so she had to stop to fill it up. Finally, on the way to school, she drove over a nail and flattened her tire. She had forgotten her cell phone, so she had to wait for an hour for help.

Effect: Keisha's carelessness resulted in more frustration. First, her teachers counted her absence as unexcused. Second, she missed an important Spanish test. Finally, the school secretary called her mother.

Example 2
Cause/effect in a list format

Cause: Sometimes overachievement in high school is due to student motivation. A highly-motivated student completes assignments and projects quickly and accurately. Another factor for overachievement is organization. An organized student is able to study and test well. The third cause for overachievement may be a supportive home environment.

Effect: Whatever the causes may be, the outlook for an overachieving student is excellent. Usually, he or she graduates from high school with top grades and a college scholarship. Most likely, this student will continue to perform well in college and in the job market.

Characteristics of the Cause/Effect Pattern

The cause/effect pattern usually includes nouns and verbs such as *cause, explanation, motive, reason, result,* and *effect.* Look at **Example 1.** Notice the word *resulted* in the second paragraph is important because it states the effects of the events in the first paragraph. The word *resulted* tells the reader to look for a cause. Look at **Example 2** again. What important word in the second paragraph tells the reader about the causes? What important word tells the reader about the effects?

Like the problem/solution pattern, the cause/effect pattern uses active verbs to signal major steps within its causes and its effects. In **Example 1,** these active verbs include *counted, missed,* and *called.*

Major steps within the cause(s) and/or effect(s) may be introduced with ordering words, such as *first, second, next,* or *finally.* Look at **Examples 1** and **2** again. There are ordering words in both examples. Can you find them?

If a reading passage is made up of actions or events and their results, in a list or in a series of steps, it is probably an example of the cause/effect pattern.

Example 3 describes a familiar cause/effect. We can tell it is a cause/effect because the word *caused* appears in the second sentence. The word *destruction* in the second sentence refers to the effects. Both the cause and the effects relate to the topic, Hurricane Thomas.

Example 3
Hurricane Thomas was devastating. Tidal waves more than 100 feet high and winds clocked at more than 100 miles per hour caused much destruction. Beaches were scattered with debris from beach homes that snapped in two. Glass shards from broken windows covered the sand. Uprooted trees lay on the beaches. Dented vehicles showed the damage resulting from hail. After the storm, residents with frayed nerves began to file damage claims.

Topic: the devastation of Hurricane Thomas
Cause: huge tidal waves and high winds
Effects: debris, glass shards, uprooted trees, dented vehicles, and nervous residents

Cause/Effect Pattern

Once you identify the cause/effect pattern in your reading, these strategies can help you read and understand the material:

1. Read the first paragraph carefully. Try to figure out the topic. Then skim the rest of the selection. Figure out how the cause, or causes, relate to the topic. Look for words like *cause, trigger, produce, motive, effect, reason, result,* and *explanation* as you read.

2. After you have figured out the topic and its causes, skim for effects. Look for phrases like *as a result, for that reason, consequently,* and *subsequently.* Then read the last paragraph carefully. See how the effects relate to the topic. Look to see if the topic has changed by the end of the reading.

3. Reread the selection. Note each cause and each effect. Look for action verbs and nouns that label minor causes within each larger cause. Look for minor effects within each larger effect. Look for adjectives that give additional details. Look for ordering words like *first, second, next, then,* or *finally.* These may list causes, effects, or details within each cause or effect.

4. Reread the first and last paragraphs. This time, look for adjectives and adverbs (descriptors) that may show an opinion. Often the first and last paragraphs state the cause(s) and effect(s) as the author sees them.

5. Try to figure out if the author's opinion is the main idea behind the cause(s) and the effect(s). See if the same viewpoint is captured in the title. Look to see if there are any descriptors showing the author's viewpoint in the title.

6. Reread the whole selection. Review the topic, each cause, and each effect related to the topic, the main idea, and the author's viewpoint.

Use the reading strategies for cause/effect patterns on page 37 to read the next passage. Then describe the topic on the line provided. Find the cause relating to the topic. Write it on the next line. Then list the effects relating to the topic.

Caring for your skin is important. Eating well helps create healthy skin. Certain foods and nutrients nourish the skin. They keep it soft and attractive. For example, fish contains oils that help maintain a good complexion. Ground flaxseeds, added to some cereals, are rich with omega-three fatty acids. These lubricate the skin. Vitamin E, found in nuts, is essential for skin repair. Vitamin A, found in dark-orange vegetables (carrots, sweet potatoes, winter squash) and dark-green vegetables (broccoli, spinach, kale) is also vital in keeping skin healthy.

Maintaining healthy skin results in other health benefits. The skin is the body's first line of defense against disease. It also protects the body's internal organs. The skin regulates body temperature. It prevents excess fluid loss, too. Finally, the skin aids the body in removing excess water and salts.

Topic: _____

Cause: _____

Effects: _____

Now apply these strategies to a longer reading. Read the next selection carefully. On the lines that follow, write the topic that is being described. While you are reading, look for descriptors that show the author's viewpoint. Identify the cause(s) and effect(s). List them all on the lines provided. There may be more than one cause/effect pattern in a long reading.

Identity theft is the malicious stealing of another person's identity. Personal information such as one's Social Security number, driver's license number, tax information, checks, or credit card number is first stolen and then used. As a result, the victim becomes subjected to a life of misery. The vicious impersonator can destroy the victim's credit and good name.

Identity theft can be caused by carelessness. Many victims do not guard their purses or wallets vigilantly. In addition to personal indentification cards and credit cards, they carry Social Security cards and cards with bank-account numbers.

Identity theft can be also caused by negligence. Many victims do not shred valuable personal information containing personal data. Tax or bank information left in the trash may fall into the wrong hands. So can bills paid by personal checks that are left in mailboxes. Personal data left in view of others at the workplace may pose another significant risk.

Finally, identity theft can be caused by lack of perception. Thieves regularly attempt to obtain personal information through scam telephone calls and e-mails. Computer hackers try to access personal information files by injecting computer viruses and accessing personal computers. If the victim fails to recognize these invasions of privacy as potential threats, he or she may become a target for identity theft.

Topic: _____

Descriptors: _____

Cause(s): _____

Effect(s): _____

The Main Idea

The main idea in the cause/effect pattern is the central statement or theme behind the cause(s) and effect(s). In short passages, the main idea may be the topic. For example, the reading about Hurricane Thomas shows how hurricanes are destructive storms.

Sometimes cause/effect patterns are written as examples for central ideas. The cause(s) and effect(s) illustrate the author's viewpoint. Thus, the author's bias is often obvious. For example, from the descriptor *devastating,* you can guess that the author views Hurricane Thomas as a threat.

Sometimes you can get a clear idea of the author's viewpoint in the first paragraph. At other times, you will need to look further. Watch for the author's use of descriptive words. These include adjectives and adverbs, but other word choices can also tell you a lot. Does the author give a reason for the causes and effects? Does the author end the passage with an overall effect? Does the author go beyond the causes and effects to make a statement? Is that statement the main idea of the selection?

Understanding the author's viewpoint will help you in several ways. If you can tell the author's viewpoint, you can weigh it for bias. You can use it to identify the main idea of a paragraph. And you can use it when you prepare a title for your outline.

Read the selection in **Example 4.** Note how the author's viewpoint can be found in the first paragraph and in the use of descriptors throughout.

Example 4

An allergy is an intense reaction within the immune system. It is a reaction to a typically harmless substance. This substance somehow causes the immune system to respond by producing large amounts of antibodies. These antibodies attach to the body's tissue and blood cells. There they trigger the release of powerful chemicals that inflame body tissue. This happens especially in the respiratory system. Allergens such as shellfish, pollen, animals, bee venom, and mold cause allergic reactions in many people.

Allergies result in many kinds of symptoms. Some symptoms, like sneezing and a runny nose, are mild but inconvenient. Others, like itching, hives, or eczema, are more disabling. In rare instances, allergic reations can lead to deadly drops in blood pressure or heart failure.

Descriptors: *intense, powerful, mild, inconvenient, disabling, deadly*
Viewpoint: Allergies are intense body reactions to certain substances.

Read the next selection. Look for the main idea. On the lines that follow, write the topic, key descriptors, and the main idea.

Sports help many people stay in shape. However, athletic competition should also promote character development. Competitive sports bring out players' character traits. Good sportsmanship results when team members act properly.

Personal integrity leads to good sportsmanship. Doing what is right is not always popular. Yet, personal honesty creates basic trust among teammates. Trust promotes friendship. Cheating, lying, and stealing do not. Reliability—doing what one has promised—supports relationships. Loyalty—putting the interests of the team above oneself—shows caring for group members.

Self-control when facing trouble also shows good sportsmanship. Courtesy, rather than anger and frustration, civilizes the game. Good behavior should be modeled by each member of the team. It shows that team membership is a privilege, not a right.

Respect for others builds good sportsmanship, too. Cooperation creates an atmosphere in which every team member feels encouraged. Players feel able to contribute to the game, no matter what their skill level. They participate both as individuals and as part of a team. Praise for a teammate's success is praise for the team.

Topic: _____

Descriptors: _____

Main Idea: _____

Titling the Reading: A Guide to the Main Idea

If a reading selection does not have a title, it is helpful to create one. This can help you identify the main idea. It will also help later when you need to give your outline a title. The title should explain the topic of the cause/effect pattern. It should also reflect the author's view of the topic. Try to keep the title short—no more than five words. The next selection tells how a species went extinct. Descriptive words tell how the author views the loss. Read the passage.

Example 5

Miss Waldron's red colobus monkey was the first primate to become extinct within the twentieth century. The species first was observed by F. Waldron in 1933. At that time, this black-and-red West African monkey lived in the rain forests of Ghana and Ivory Coast.

Sensitive to change, this species depended on a stable environment. Loggers and farmers, however, altered the environment. This reduced the monkeys' food supply. Unchecked hunters killed many of the remaining monkeys. As a result, the species decreased.

In 1978, the monkeys were last sighted in the rain forest of Ghana. In 1988, the species was placed on the endangered list. Between 1993 and 1999, anthropologists from the Wildlife Conservation Society searched unsuccessfully for the species. Instead, they found signs of uncontrolled hunting: hunting camps, shotgun shells, and snare traps.

Although this type of monkey has vanished, a valuable lesson may be learned from the loss. Unless strict laws are passed to protect forested areas, and unless humans are better controlled, other species, here today, will be gone forever.

The adjectives *valuable* and *strict* show the author's view about laws needed to protect other species. A title like "Another Valuable Preservation Lesson" reflects the author's viewpoint.

Titling Strategies

Sometimes it is easy to think of a title. At other times, you may need to use a system. If you cannot think of a title, try "building" one with these steps:

1. Use words such as *cause(s), reason(s), effect(s),* and *result(s)* in your title.

2. Add a descriptor (adjective or adverb) that reflects the main idea.

3. Limit your title to five words.

Activity 18

Read the selection below. Identify the cause/effect pattern. While you read, look for descriptors that show the author's viewpoint or bias. Then title the selection. Write the topic, key descriptors, and your title on the lines that follow the reading.

Tornadoes are the most deadly, destructive storms on earth. During an average year, hundreds of tornadoes occur. They result in injuries and deaths. Tornadoes usually happen in the spring and summer. However, they can occur at other times, too.

Tornadoes are violent, rotating columns of air. They extend from a thunderstorm to the ground. Known as funnels, these columns move over land. They cause great damage where they descend. Spinning clockwise in the Southern Hemisphere and counterclockwise in the Northern Hemisphere, these twisters move over land randomly.

The exact causes of tornadoes are not completely known. However, they have something to do with motion in the atmosphere. The movement of warm and cold fronts is key to creating unstable weather. This sets the conditions for tornadoes. As cold fronts advance, thunderstorms develop within the warm, moist air. Changing wind direction, along with increased wind speed, creates horizontal spinning in the lower atmosphere. The spinning becomes vertical as the air rises. These cyclones are formed of wall clouds that rotate for two to six miles. They move unpredictably with varying wind speeds.

Typically, tornadoes produce large, damaging hail. Most of the destruction, though, depends on wind speed. The Fujita Tornado Damage Scale rates tornadoes based on wind speed (in miles per hour) from F0 (less than 73 mph) to F5 (261–318 mph). In 1985, an F5 tornado, clocked at 300 miles per hour, hit western Pennsylvania. Catastrophic storms like this cyclone hit less frequently. Yet, they result in phenomenal damage to property. They also cause injuries and fatalities.

Topic: _____

Descriptors: _____

Title: _____

Recognizing Causes and Effects

The cause/effect pattern in longer readings usually consists of a list of causes and effects that appear in order. The order usually follows a special sequence or rank. Each major cause may include a set of minor causes with their own details. Each major effect may include a set of minor effects with their own details. Readers need to distinguish between the major and minor causes and effects.

The example below lists the effects of the Great William Sound earthquake. Each effect includes several minor effects. These minor effects can be called primary details. Information about each minor effect (primary detail) can be called minor details.

Example 6

To date, the Great Prince William Sound earthquake has been recorded as the largest American earthquake. It hit the Anchorage, Alaska, area on March 27, 1964, at 5:36 P.M. local time. The epicenter was six miles east of College Fiord.

This earthquake was the second-largest recorded earthquake in the world. It measured 9.2 on the Richter scale. Although it lasted for only four minutes, shockwaves traveled throughout the earth. Thousands of aftershocks were recorded as far away as Texas, Florida, Cuba, and Puerto Rico.

The cause of the earthquake was a 30-foot shift of the Pacific plate under the North American plate. Uplifts, or upward thrusts of earth, affected a 200,000-square-mile area. Nearby, the Latouche Island area shifted about 60 feet to the southeast.

> **Major Cause:** shift of Pacific plate
> **Major Effect:** uplifts
> **Minor Effect (Primary Detail):** shifting of Latouche Island

Property damage in the Anchorage area was devastating. Anchorage was about 75 miles from the epicenter. It sustained the most damage. Businesses, schools, and homes were destroyed. Landslides broke the ground. Water mains, gas lines, sewers, and telephone and electrical systems were affected. Overall, the damage was estimated at $300–400 million in 1964 dollars.

> **Major Effect:** property damage
> **Minor Effect (Primary Detail):** water, gas, sewers, telephone, electrical systems damaged
> **Minor Detail:** damage estimated at $300–400 million in 1964 dollars

The uplift also resulted in movement of the ocean floor. This created the second-largest tsunami ever recorded. Seismic waves caused vertical motions that were felt as far away as Texas and Florida. These long seismic waves traveled the earth for weeks.

> **Major Effect:** movement of ocean floor
> **Minor Effect (Primary Detail):** created seismic waves
> **Minor Detail:** vertical motions felt in Texas and Florida

The earthquake created hazardous living conditions. However, most of the recorded 115 deaths were caused by flooding. Flooding was the result of high ocean waves and the movement of the ocean floor. Waves in the Anchorage area were estimated at 230 feet tall. They claimed at least 82 lives.

> **Major Effect:** deaths
> **Minor Effect (Primary Detail):** death by flooding
> **Minor Detail:** waves estimated at 230 feet claimed at least 82 lives

Unlike shorter readings, longer cause/effect passages may be challenging. You may need to combine several minor causes or effects and rename them. Of course, you will still need to keep track of the minor causes and effects. They will be the supporting details in your outline.

The example below describes the training required for successful mountain climbing. The major cause consists of minor causes (primary details). You do not need to remember all the primary details or related minor details to understand the major cause. However, some primary detail should be recalled.

Example 7
Mountain climbing is an exciting sport. Some mountain climbers climb on their own. They make their own plans and follow their own agendas. Others choose to join expeditions. They make reservations to join a specific climb. Mountaineering schools and expedition companies offer equipment rentals. They also offer the services of guided tours. These are costly, but they provide the chance to ascend the world's highest peaks.

Both private and guided mountain-climbing teams demand top physical condition in their members. Climbers need strength and endurance for maximum climbing potential. Each climber's success and the team's overall safety depend on physical conditioning. As a result, climbers-in-training must work hard to reach their top fitness levels. Successful mountain climbing demands it.

> **Major Cause:** fitness training for mountain climbers

First, hopeful climbers should check with their doctors before starting strenuous endurance training. If approved, they should start with cardiovascular conditioning. This is key to overall strength training. A well-conditioned body carries blood and oxygen to the muscles. Good circulation increases the body's capacity to work harder. Cardiovascular conditioning includes aerobic activities. They should be sustained for at least 45 minutes. These activities include running, bicycling, and stair-stepping.

Minor Cause (Primary Detail): cardiovascular conditioning
Minor Details: aerobic activities—running, bicycling, stair-stepping

Also, prospective climbers should begin strength conditioning. A personal trainer and a weight-machine program will help climbers reach their maximum strength potential.

Minor Cause (Primary Detail): strength conditioning
Minor Details: personal trainer and weight-machine program

Finally, climbers-in-training should increase their physical fitness levels with climbing simulations. To do so, they should hike steep outdoor trails. They should ascend over 3,500 feet while carrying a 55- to 60-pound pack. Prospective climbers should also regularly use a stair-stepping machine while training with heavy packs and boots.

Minor Cause (Primary Detail): simulated mountain climbing
Minor Details: hike steep outdoor trails, use stair-stepping machine with heavy packs and boots

The overall mountain-climbing experience depends on the climber's preconditioning level. A strong, well-conditioned body will perform better. Its blood vessels will carry needed blood and oxygen to the body extremities as needed. A higher physical fitness level also allows the climber to adjust to changes in altitude levels. In dangerous situations, endurance levels may even decide the climber's survival.

Word Clues

Ordering words such as *first, second, third, next, also,* and *finally* are important. They can help readers spot major causes and effects, primary details, and minor details within the cause/effect pattern. Action verbs that label primary and minor details offer additional clues. Words like *cause(s), motive, reason, effect(s), explanation,* and *result,* and phrases like *for that reason, consequently,* and *subsequently* show the cause/effect pattern. They introduce major causes and effects and their supporting details.

Here is another passage on hiking. The minor effects (primary details) are usually introduced with ordering words. Read the selection carefully. Note the word clues.

Example 8
Private organizations and government agencies are concerned about threats to our mountain environments. Mountain ecologies are being damaged by unregulated backpacking and hiking.

> **Major Cause:** threatened mountain environments
> **Minor Cause (Primary Detail):** unregulated backpacking and hiking
> **Word Clues:** *concerned, unregulated*

Together, these groups promote conservation and preservation. They often preach the following "commandments."

> **Major Effect:** conservation/preservation

First, backpackers and hikers should plan and prepare ahead. They should know the mountain terrain and the ecology of the local area. They should understand high-altitude weather. Backpackers and hikers should know their route and their equipment. Secondly, hikers should leave plants, rocks, and other objects alone. Fires should be made only in permitted areas, and only dead wood should be burned. Fires should never be unattended. Next, backpackers and hikers should travel and camp on hard surfaces, such as rock. They should use only designated sites and should avoid untraveled areas. When they must camp on vegetation, they should select thick, grassy sites. Finally, backpackers and hikers must carry out all their trash. They should not leave anything behind. They must dispose of organic waste by digging holes and burying it. They should not pollute stream water. Water should be carried 200 feet from streams for washing. Campers should scatter used dishwater. In other words, they should leave the area as they found it.

> **Minor Effects (Primary Details):** plan and prepare ahead; leave nature alone; travel and camp in designated areas; dispose of trash; use water away from streams; leave area as they found it
> **Word Clues:** *"commandments," first, secondly, next, finally*

Read the following selection. Try to identify the topic. On the lines that follow, name one major cause and one major effect. Rename minor effects as broadly as possible. These will become primary details. You may find it helpful to underline the word clues in each paragraph.

Tsunamis are often described as tidal waves. This is not accurate. Tsunamis are not caused by the tidal action of the moon and sun. They are caused by sudden vertical movement of the ocean floor during an earthquake. The effect of the earthquake cannot be seen right away in water that is three miles deep. However, the altered water waves can travel distances of more that 430 miles. As tsunamis reach the shore, wave heights can reach 80 feet.

Topic: _____

Major Cause: _____

Major Effect: _____

Areas in the United States vary in seismic activity. The North American East Coast does not have vertical fault displacement. Thus, seismic activity in the eastern United States is low compared with other regions in the country. For example, no tsunami occurred during the Charleston earthquake in 1886. This was a notable American earthquake. The only tsunami recorded on the Atlantic Coast of North America occurred in 1929 off Burin Peninsula, Newfoundland.

Minor Effect (Primary Detail): _____

Minor Detail: _____

In contrast with the East Coast, the Pacific West Coast has been affected by a number of tsunamis. They are generated by South American and Alaskan earthquakes. In particular, the 1964 Alaskan quake produced 20-foot waves in California. The result was $7.5 million in damage and 11 deaths. The coasts of Oregon and Washington also sustained high waves.

Minor Effect (Primary Detail): _____

Minor Detail: _____

Although the West has been affected by earthquake activity, Alaska is really the source of many major earthquakes and tsunamis. Alaska rests on both the Pacific and North American tectonic plates. As the plates collide, fault lines become vertically displaced. This creates volatile seismic activity. Due to the unstable conditions, four major tsunamis have been generated in Alaska. They have resulted in many fatalities and great property damage.

Minor Effect (Primary Detail): _____

Minor Detail: _____

The Hawaiian Islands also have sustained many destructive tsunamis. This is mainly due to their location in the Pacific Ocean, where about 90 percent of all recorded tsunamis occur. Tsunamis caused by both local and distant sources have affected the fiftieth state. The worst tsunamis occurred in 1869 and in 1975. They produced waves up to 59 feet high.

Minor Effect (Primary Detail): _____

Minor Detail: _____

Using a Graphic Organizer

A graphic organizer like the one that follows can help you prepare for making an outline. At the top of the organizer, label the topic. Then list each major cause within the cause diagram. Write the primary details (minor causes) below each major cause. Do the same thing for the major effects and their primary details (minor effects). Fill in only the important minor details. The completed organizer should give you a clear overview of the cause/effect pattern.

Topic:

Major Cause #1:	**Major Cause #2:**
Minor Causes: 1. 2.	**Minor Causes:** 1. 2.
Minor Details:	**Minor Details:**

Major Effect #1:	**Major Effect #2:**
Minor Effects: 1. 2.	**Minor Effects:** 1. 2.
Minor Details:	**Minor Details:**

Major Cause #3:   **Major Cause #4:**

Minor Causes: **Minor Causes:**
 1.   1.

 2.   2.

Minor Details: **Minor Details:**

Major Effect #3:   **Major Effect #4:**

Minor Effects: **Minor Effects:**
 1.   1.

 2.   2.

Minor Details: **Minor Details:**

Designing the Cause/Effect Pattern Outline

In the cause/effect outline, there is a Roman-numeral heading for each general cause and general effect. Each major cause and each major effect then gets a capital-letter entry. Each minor cause or effect (primary detail) gets an Arabic-numeral entry. Any minor detail pertaining to a minor cause or effect is a lowercase-letter entry. As always, the outline moves from general to specific as the entries move from left to right. **Example 8** discussed the work of conservationists. Here is what an outline based on that example might look like:

Preserving the Mountain

    I. Threatened mountain environments
        A. Unregulated hiking
        B. Unregulated backpacking
    II. Conservation/preservation "commandments"
        A. Plan and prepare ahead
            1. Know terrain
            2. Understand weather
            3. Know route
            4. Know equipment
        B. Leave nature alone
        C. Travel/camp on hard surfaces in designated areas
        D. Dispose of waste and trash
            1. Carry out trash
            2. Dig holes for organic waste
            3. Do not pollute water
                a. Carry wash water 200 feet from stream
                b. Scatter used dishwater

Building a Cause/Effect Outline

To build a cause/effect outline, you need to combine the steps you have learned in this chapter. You may want to use the graphic organizer to record the information you gather. When the organizer is completed, use it to fill in your outline.

1. Use the general cause as the first Roman-numeral heading. If you cannot think of a good title, use the word *causes* as your first Roman-numeral heading. Then use the general effect as the second Roman-numeral heading. You can also use the word *effects* as your second Roman-numeral heading.

2. List each major cause and effect as a capital-letter entry.

3. When there are minor causes, list at least two under their major cause. Likewise, if there are minor effects, list at least two under their major effect. Give these Arabic-numeral entries.

4. When there are minor details, list at least two under their minor cause or minor effect. Give these lowercase-letter entries. Unless the minor details are important, you probably will not need to add them to your outline.

5. Finally, title your outline. Try to capture the author's view of the topic. Use no more than five words.

Following the steps listed on page 53, make a short outline for the next reading. Do not use more than two Roman-numeral headings.

During the last quarter of the twentieth century, the mortality rate in the United States has declined. In other words, older Americans are living longer. Improved medical treatment, lack of widespread disease, and good eating and exercise habits are often cited as reasons. At any rate, younger Americans have become outnumbered as the baby boomers approach their golden years.

Because the ratio of young to old has *declined,* funding for the Social Security system has been threatened. Incoming wages no longer match outgoing payments in benefits. The Social Security system has therefore been changed.

In 1983, Congress altered the system by increasing the retirement age. Instead of receiving their full, lifelong monthly benefit at 65, American workers were assigned two more working years. Future American retirees would become eligible for full benefits at age 67.

A delayed retirement age has many effects. First, older Americans must work longer or face reduced retirement benefits. Second, because many seniors depend on Social Security for at least half of their post-retirement income, the physical ability to work longer has become a key issue. Third, health insurance represents another real concern. Because senior Americans must be 65 before qualifying for Medicare, many older Americans look for post-retirement jobs. They are seeking full medical benefits until they can qualify for federal assistance.

Finally, early retirement, once a common occurrence, may no longer be an easy option. Careful financial planning throughout one's working years is now necessary for a comfortable retirement.

Outline Title: _____

   I.   _____

      A. _____

         1._____

         2._____

         3._____

      B. _____

  II. _____

      A. _____

      B. _____

      C. _____

      D. _____

Practice your skills with this longer reading selection. Follow the same steps as you did in Activity 20. This time, however, make your own outline on a separate sheet of paper. Use no more than two Roman-numeral headings. Remember, proper outline style means that you should not have just one capital-letter and/or Arabic-numeral entry. You must have at least two under any given heading.

The West Nile virus has emerged recently. It presents a threat to public and animal health. In 1937, the virus was isolated in a feverish adult woman living in the West Nile District of Uganda. By the 1950s, the virus was recognized as a cause of human encephalitis. This is a deadly inflammation of the spinal cord and brain. Since 1999, encephalitis in North America has been associated with the West Nile virus. Hundreds of cases of encephalitis linked to the West Nile virus have been reported to the Centers for Disease Control and Prevention (CDC). Many cases have been fatal.

The West Nile virus is transmitted to animals through mosquito bites. Birds are especially affected. They carry high virus levels in their bloodstream. Infected crows react immediately to the West Nile virus. This helps health authorities determine the severity of the virus outbreak. A high death rate among crows usually signals the presence of the West Nile virus.

Mosquitoes may also inject the virus into the blood of humans. The effect of the West Nile virus on humans can be West Nile encephalitis, a severe illness. While most West Nile–infected humans have no symptoms, some sufferers may develop mild symptoms. These can include fever, headache, body aches, skin rash, and swollen glands. A smaller percentage of infected people develop more severe illness, including meningitis or full-blown encephalitis. These are marked by high fever, neck stiffness, stupor, coma, tremors or convulsions, muscle weakness, and paralysis. Fatality rates range from 3 to 15 percent. Death rates are highest among the elderly.

Prompt medical care should be sought for such symptoms. Treatment may include hospitalization, intravenous fluids, and nutrition and respiratory support, especially in severe cases.

Currently, no vaccine exists to fight the West Nile virus. The best prevention is avoiding mosquito contact. This is an added risk during summer dawn and dusk hours. Reducing outdoor activity during these times can help. However, if one must be outside then, using insect repellent and wearing a long-sleeved shirt and a pair of pants is the safest choice.

Recognizing the Pattern

The **comparison/contrast** pattern is easy to identify. Two or more items, actions, people, or ideas are compared. Their differences or similarities are pointed out. You can find this two-part pattern in articles discussing different points of view. It is used to examine the various sides of controversial issues. In school, the comparison/contrast pattern is often found in social studies textbooks. It also appears in psychology, science, and literature selections.

In the comparison/contrast pattern, two or more things sharing common points are placed side by side. Their common points are the basis of the pattern. Comparisons center on both similarities and differences between items. Contrasts stress the opposites between items. Look at **Example 1.** Note that the word *opposite* is used in the contrast paragraph.

Example 1

Comparison: A grape and an olive are both small, elliptical fruits. Yet they are quite different. A grape tastes sweet and is eaten as a dessert or snack. An olive, on the other hand, tastes savory and is usually eaten as a condiment.

Contrast: A grape and an olive are opposite in taste and use. A grape is sweet, but the olive is savory. A grape is eaten as a snack or dessert; the olive is eaten as a condiment or in a salad.

Characteristics of the Comparison/Contrast Pattern

The order of the items being compared and contrasted is very important. In **Example 1,** first the grape, then the olive are presented. The order of the points of comparison is also important.

In the **item-by-item** contrast below, note how the points of comparison are made first for the month of July, then for January. The points are made in the same order in the first and second paragraphs.

Example 2

July, the seventh month of the year, occurs during the hot summer months. This month typically has high temperatures, ranging from the high 80s to over 100 degrees. July is steamy—good for outdoor, water-related sports.

January, the first month of the year, occurs during the cold winter months. This month typically has low temperatures, ranging from below zero to 30 degrees. January is frigid—good for indoor games and other activities.

Item-by-item comparisons or contrasts occur often in readings that follow this pattern. However, you may sometimes see a **point-by-point** comparison or contrast. Note that in **Example 3,** the two things being compared/contrasted are discussed at the same time, as each point of comparison is introduced. The items are listed in the corresponding order:

Example 3
The months of January and July are opposite in many respects. First, these months occur in opposite seasons: January during the winter, July during the summer. In temperature, January is frigid, with temperatures ranging from below zero to 30 degrees. July, on the other hand, is scorching, with temperatures ranging from the upper 80s to over 100 degrees. Finally, different activities are suited to each month. January is great for indoor games and activities; July is perfect for outdoor, water-related sports.

Sentence structure is important in building comparisons. Sentences that discuss one item correspond to sentences that discuss the other item(s). Good sentence structure plays a big part in making the overall pattern strong.

Words also can help make comparisons strong. Nouns and verbs such as *advantage, disadvantage, difference, comparison, variation, contrast, opposite, differ, contrast, compare,* and *oppose* signal comparisons. Look back at **Example 3.** Notice the word *opposite* in the first sentence. It is important because it signals a contrast. Now look at the first paragraph of **Example 1.** Can you find another important word?

Other words and phrases like *but, however, nevertheless, on the contrary, on the other hand,* and *in contrast* also are important. They, too, show that items are being compared. In **Example 3,** *on the other hand* is used to contrast July with January.

Finally, ordering words like *first, second, next,* or *finally* may introduce points within the comparison. Look at **Example 3** again. See how the ordering words (*first, finally*) work to introduce points. Now look at **Example 1.** There are no ordering words. When do you think ordering words are necessary?

If a reading passage examines two or more things by showing how they are alike as well as different, and if the things are examined in a logical order, the passage is probably in the comparison/contrast pattern.

The paragraph in **Example 4** compares past and present lifestyles. We can recognize it as a comparison because the phrase *in comparison* appears in the first sentence of the second paragraph. Note how sentence structure works to introduce similar points in each paragraph.

Example 4

The 1950s marked the birth of television. This revolutionary box brought images into American homes that had formerly relied on the sounds of radio. At first it was considered a luxury. Soon, however, the television's black-and-white screen mesmerized school-age children. Television shows increased. Programs such as *I Love Lucy* became a part of American life.

In comparison, the 1990s ushered in the networked computer. This new technology began to challenge the importance of color television in American homes. At first, it was considered too complex. Yet, the computer's capacity to communicate across the world soon awed Americans. Computer sales soared. Application programs and Internet search engines became household words.

> **Comparison:** 1950s and 1990s technology
> **Items of comparison:** television, computer/Internet
> **Points:** revolutionary aspect of item, effects of item on people, use of item

Once you identify the comparison/contrast pattern in your reading, these strategies can help you read and understand the material:

Comparison/Contrast Pattern

1. Read the first paragraph carefully. Figure out the overall comparison. Find out the purpose for the comparison. Skim the rest of the selection to see how the comparison is made.

2. Read the last paragraph carefully. Verify the purpose for the comparison. Figure out why the comparison has been made.

3. Read the whole selection. Look for items and points in the comparison. Are there opposites? Note how sentence structure is used to present points. Do the sentences parallel each other? Is the comparison tight or loose? Notice how the minor points support each major point.

4. Notice how key words support the comparison. Look for nouns and verbs that show comparison. Examples include *advantage, difference, disadvantage, comparison, variation, contrast, opposite, differ, contrast, compare,* and *opposite.* Look for words and phrases like *but, however, nevertheless, on the contrary, on the other hand,* and *in contrast.* Also, look for ordering words like *first, second,* and *finally.* These may introduce each point within the comparison. Finally, look for descriptive words that may name items being compared, points of comparison, and supporting details.

5. Reread the selection. Pay close attention to the first paragraph to find out what the author is saying about the comparison. This is the main idea of the selection.

6. Continue reading. Look for descriptors (adjectives and adverbs) that supports the author's opinion. Read the last paragraph to see if the main idea is restated. See if the title also reflects the author's viewpoint.

7. Review the purpose for the comparison, the items being compared, the points in the comparison, the main idea, and the title.

Read the next selection. Follow the reading strategies described on page 60. Then, on the lines that follow, describe what the comparison is, the items being compared, and the points of comparison.

The fashion of the 1950s reflected the rigid standards of the time. Being dressed up was considered proper. Teenage girls wore knee-length skirts or dresses to school. Especially popular were circular skirts and poodle skirts. Pants and jeans were not considered proper dress for girls. Short shorts were never worn. Instead, many girls wore flared, knee-length Bermuda shorts and long capri pants called "pedal pushers."

In contrast to the 1950s, American dress today has no overall standard. Individual tastes, not society at large, determine what is proper. Teenage girls wear comfortable jeans and shorts in a variety of lengths to school. Especially popular are low-cut jeans. Skirts and dresses are rarely worn. Instead, many girls wear dress pants in many styles and materials.

Overall Comparison:_____

Items Compared: _____

Points:_____

Now try applying this approach to a longer passage. Use the reading strategies described on page 60. Read the selection carefully. Then, on the lines below, describe the comparison, the items being compared, and the points of comparison.

Life in the 1950s was very different from our present life. Society in the postwar '50s expected people to behave alike. Instead of having many different social behaviors and lifestyles, people tended to live just like their neighbors.

Men's clothing during the 1950s reflected a uniform style. Clothing reflected a man's role as the primary breadwinner and head of household. Men's subdued, formal clothing lacked variety and color. Men who dressed for work were expected to wear the "correct" outfit: a charcoal gray, blue, or brown business suit. A white shirt and tie were also musts. Finally, most men were expected to wear hats.

Boys' dress reflected men's clothing. They did not wear jeans or shorts to school. The "preppy" look was in. Instead, boys wore dress pants and sweaters. Letter sweaters were popular dress items. Shirts made to hang out were the only flexible dress article allowed in school.

Reflecting today's diverse society, men's clothing now suggests a shared role at work and at home. Men's clothing, like men's roles within their families, varies. Casual dress has become preferred over the business suit. It is characterized by many styles, fabrics, and colors. A shirt and tie are worn together only if desired. Hats also have become casual. Today, the baseball cap tops the formal hat in popularity.

Today's boys do not look like little men. Instead, they have their own identity and look. The look centers on comfortable jeans, shorts, and shirts. Dress pants and sweaters usually are not worn to school. For the most part, casual wear in a variety of styles and colors has become accepted as school dress.

Overall Comparison:_____

Items Compared: _____

Points: _____

The Main Idea

The main idea in the comparison/contrast pattern is the central statement or theme behind the comparison. For example, the passage in Activity 23 was written to show how fashion may reflect social behavior. Comparison between items (men's and boys' clothes in the 1950s versus those of today) provides support for central ideas. Sometimes the author's viewpoint is obvious within that central idea.

The author may choose to create a tight comparison. This involves sentences that show point-by-point contrasts between items. This kind of comparison is made in the previous examples. These tightly-drawn comparisons are usually short, and they can be tedious. On the other hand, the author may choose to compare items more loosely. The passage may not include all the points for every item within the comparison.

In either case, without a main idea, any comparison becomes a list of facts. A comparison is usually designed to support the author's viewpoint. Therefore, the way the author presents the information is important. Sometimes you can find a clear idea of the author's viewpoint in the first paragraph. At other times, you will need to look further. You should look at the author's use of descriptive words. These descriptors are mostly adjectives and adverbs, but other word choices can tell you a lot. For example, note the descriptor *"correct"* in the second paragraph of Activity 23. You can guess that the author probably disagrees that all men should have to dress alike in the workplace.

Understanding the author's opinion will help you in several ways. If you know the author's viewpoint, you can weigh it for bias. You can use it to identify the main idea of a paragraph. You can also use it later when you need a title for your outline.

As you read the next selection, note how the author's viewpoint can be found in the first and last paragraphs.

Example 5
Colors affect emotions and moods. Certain colors produce psychological reactions that either stimulate or soothe us. It is useful to know how most people react to contrasting colors. It can help in creating desirable atmospheres.

Active colors such as yellow, orange, and red arouse us. These warm colors brighten and inspire us. They evoke positive attitudes. Active colors should be used in activity rooms, such as kitchens, offices, and study areas. Red, the most intense of the group, produces the greatest emotional response. Its force heats up a room. Oranges and yellows produce a milder effect. They cheer, energize, and refresh.

On the other hand, passive colors such as blue, green, and purple soothe us. These cooling colors calm and reenergize us. They evoke tranquility. Passive colors should be used in rooms used for rest and relaxation, such as bedrooms, living rooms, and family rooms. Greens produce stability and security; they connect us to nature. Blues and purples bring serenity, mystery, and reflection. They comfort and content us.

Neutralizers, or "uncolors," include browns, beiges, taupes, grays, and white. They do not evoke much emotional response. They neither activate nor pacify us. Instead, they serve to bridge our moods between colors and rooms. Neutralizers are good colors for neutral areas like kitchens or baths. Neutralizers combine and cooperate. White especially can make spaces look larger. It also complements other colors.

Since we respond emotionally to different colors, color is important in creating a particular atmosphere. Color combinations can exhilarate our senses. They add another psychological dimension to our everyday lives.

Descriptors (last paragraph): *emotionally, particular, exhilarate, psychological*
Viewpoint: Color environments are important. They can produce a desirable
emotional response.

Read the selection below. Look for the main idea. On the lines that follow, describe the overall comparison, key descriptors, and the main idea. Note the loose sentence construction in this reading.

According to a study done for Edy's Grand Ice Cream, ice cream flavors can be linked to different personalites. The study may not be totally accurate. However, the unique findings present a clever sales pitch. Of the Americans polled, 27% chose chocolate, 22% selected vanilla, 21% picked chocolate chip, 16% preferred strawberries with cream, and 9% favored butter pecan.

According to the study, vanilla lovers enjoy close family relationships. They are impulsive risk-takers. They possess big goals and high self-expectations. Vanilla lovers get along only with other vanilla lovers.

Chocolate cravers enjoy being the center of attention. They are the life of the party and hate routine. They are lively, creative people who are also charming and enthusiastic. Chocolate lovers are fond of butter-pecan or chocolate-chip lovers.

Butter-pecan fans are orderly perfectionists. They are conservative and careful. Moral and conscientious, they are also very competitive in sports. These people have take-charge personalities. Butter-pecan lovers are attracted to chocolate, chocolate-chip, and other butter-pecan types.

Those who adore strawberries and cream are introverted and opinionated. They are self-critical and detail-oriented. Yet, they are strong emotionally. Lovers of strawberries and cream get along with chocolate-chip fans.

Finally, those who go for chocolate chip are able and ambitious. These people are accomplished, generous, and competitive. They also are charming and skilled in social situations. Chocolate-chip lovers are comfortable with chocolate, butter-pecan, and strawberry fans.

Comparison: _____

Descriptors: _____

Main Idea: _____

Titling the Reading: A Guide to the Main Idea

If a reading selection does not have a title, it is helpful to create one. This can help you identify the main idea. It will also help later when you need to give your outline a title. The title should explain the comparison/contrast. It should also reflect the author's view of the topic. Try to keep it short—no more than five words. The next selection describes a familiar comparison: looking at preowned cars to buy. Note the use of descriptors that show the author's opinion.

Example 6

Selecting a preowned car can be frustrating. This is especially true when money is an issue. If money is a problem, the buyer must balance the price of the vehicle with its mileage, year, and overall condition.

Buying a used car with over 50,000 miles is smart as far as price is concerned. The high-mileage vehicles are usually lower in price. Whether or not the car works well, though, may depend on how long it has been driven. Its year and model may give additional clues. Less visible evidence depends on where the car has been driven. Finally, how well the previous owner cared for the car will show in its performance.

On the other hand, buying a newer preowned car with less than 50,000 miles may be smarter. True, the price of newer used models is higher than that of older used cars. However, newer cars tend to require fewer repairs. Still, buyers must beware when purchasing any preowned car. A preowned car is a good deal only if it works.

The adjectives *frustrating, less visible, well,* and *good deal,* show the author's concern about buying a used car. A title such as "Selecting a Working Used Car" reflects the author's viewpoint.

Titling Strategies

Sometimes it is easy to think of a title for a reading. At other times, you may need to use a system. If you cannot think of a title, try to "build" one by following these steps:

1. Use words like *contrast, comparison, similar, like, different, unlike,* or *opposite* in your title.

2. Add nouns or adjectives that show the author's view of the comparison/contrast.

3. Limit your title to five words.

Read the passsage below. Identify the comparison that is being made. Look for descriptors that show the author's viewpoint or bias. Then create a title for the selection. On the lines below the reading, tell what is being compared. Also, write down key descriptors and your title.

The Seven Summits include the largest mountain on each of the seven continents. One of these mountains, Vinson Massif, is the highest peak in Antarctica. It is located within the Sentinel Range of the Ellsworth Mountains. It measures a massive 13 miles long and 8 miles wide. Although Vinson Massif itself is not considered a dangerous climb, the weather is problematic. Severe Antarctic weather conditions are a concern for mountain climbers. First ascended in 1966 by an American team, this large mountain measures 16,066 feet high.

In contrast, Mount Kilimanjaro is the highest peak in Africa. Located near the Tanzania-Kenya border, Mount Kilimanjaro sits amid the scrub lands and beautiful, lush forests. Once an active volcano, the mountain now towers over the Tanzanian plains. Kibo, a summit crater, and Mawenzi, a secondary peak, share its summit. First ascended in 1889, this spectacular mountain is 19,340 feet high.

Comparison: _____

Descriptors: _____

Title: _____

Recognizing Items and Points of Comparison

In longer readings, the comparison/contrast pattern is usually made up of items and points of comparison. Points of comparison include supporting details. Sometimes the supporting details can be confusing. Readers must distinguish between the points of comparison and the details that support those points.

The example below compares four temperament types (items). They are compared according to types of behavior (points or primary details). Supporting details (minor details) list these personality traits. You do not need to remember all the personality traits to spot each personality type. However, you do need to link each temperament type with at least one behavior.

Example 7
Myers-Briggs Type Indicators and the Keirsey Temperament Sorter are used in business. These tools encourage compatibility and productivity among workers. They can also help people make career choices. Both instruments are used to measure personality types.

Both tools use four basic scales. They measure extraversion/introversion, sensate/intuitive, thinking/feeling, and judging/perceiving. From these measures, people are grouped into four basic personality types. These contrasting types show a variety of characteristics and behaviors.

The first type is the fun-loving artisan. These people are optimistic, unconventional, and spontaneous. Artisans love action and variety. They resist being confined and wish to go as they please. Artisans enjoy the present and do not think much about the future.

> **Item:** the fun-loving artisan
> **Point (Primary Detail):** lover of action and variety
> **Supporting Details (Minor Details):** optimisitic, unconventional, spontaneous, resist being confined

The second type is the dependable, practical guardian. These people are predictable and steady. They are self-disciplined and work-oriented. Guardians keep society stable. They maintain order and keep things working. Guardians look before they leap.

> **Item:** the dependable, practical guardian
> **Point (Primary Detail):** self-disciplined, work-oriented
> **Supportive Details (Minor Details):** predictable and steady, maintain order

The third type is the politically correct reasoner. These people are independent and practical. They are problem solvers and lovers of logic. A reasoner is an innovator.

> **Item:** the politically correct reasoner
> **Point (Primary Detail):** problem solver and lover of logic
> **Supporting Details (Minor Details):** independent, practical, innovator

The final type is the ethical idealist. These people are kindhearted, noble, and loving. They seek self-improvement and strive to help others achieve their potential. These generous, trusting people inspire the world to love and care about others.

> **Item:** the ethical idealist
> **Point (Primary Detail):** seek self-improvement and strive to help others
> **Supporting Details (Minor Details):** kindhearted, noble, loving, generous, trusting

Longer comparison/contrast readings may be more difficult. Often you may have to recombine points and supporting details for clarity. Of course, you will still need to keep track of the minor points. These will be the supporting details in your outline.

The next example compares past and present fire-prevention methods. To understand the comparison, the reader needs to understand how past and present policies differ. Note how the items of comparison, wildfires regulated by controlled burning versus wildfire prevention (no burning), are supported by points of comparison and supporting detail.

Example 8

Wildfires have become a controversial issue. In the past, wildfires regulated by controlled-burning policies were viewed as a natural phenomenon. Wildfires were not viewed as a threat because large populations did not exist in rural western areas.

Therefore, controlled-burning policies were freely practiced. These policies, adopted in the 1970s by the National Park Service, were known as the "let-burn" policies. These controlled-burning policies allowed the use of wildfires to set boundary controls. Existing fuels also could be burned under certain conditions. Another acceptable policy was the "least-cost-plus-loss" procedure. This practice determined the amount of fire control by the amount of damage prevented. Because most wildfires occurred naturally from lightning, they tended to cause little damage. In unpopulated areas, they were simply left to burn.

But now wildfires, even those regulated by controlled burning, are viewed differently. The growth of larger populations in rural western states has changed public perception of wildfires. Many people now view wildfires negatively. Wildfires pose a threat to the businesses and homes that have sprouted up in heavily-wooded, rural western areas. As a result, federal and state fire-prevention laws have been enacted. Wildfires, prohibited by law, now require the services of firefighters and a variety of costly equipment. Wildfires have become another national disaster.

> **Items:** controlled-burning policies, wildfire prevention (no burning)
> **Points (Primary Details):** perception, population, policies
> **Supporting Details (Minor Details):** "let-burn" policies; "least-cost-plus-loss" policy; federal and state wildfire prevention laws; firefighters; costly equipment

Word Clues

Words and phrases like *but, however, nevertheless, on the contrary, on the other hand*, and *in contrast* signal that items are being compared. Words like *differ, contrast, difference, comparison, opposing, advantage*, and *disadvantage* may also be used to compare items. Ordering words such as *first, second, next*, or *finally* will help you recognize points within the comparison. Sometimes descriptive words can also help you identify points within the comparison and supporting details.

The next example compares two substances in the bloodstream. Each substance is introduced by an ordering word. Read the selection carefully. Look for both the items and points of comparison. Then note the word clues.

Example 9

Fats in the diet are absorbed and transported by lipids in the blood. As food is metabolized, lipoproteins are created. These are categorized by density, or the ratio of protein and fats. As the food is absorbed, lipoproteins move from the liver to blood vessels. There they are either absorbed or bound to the blood vessel walls.

Cholesterol is a lipoprotein complex. It is made by the liver, where it enters the bloodstream. The total amount of cholesterol in the bloodstream is usually referred to as one's cholesterol level. This is measured by the ratio of contrasting components in cholesterol.

The first component is LDL (low-density lipoproteins). LDL is considered bad cholesterol. A high-carbohydrate diet raises LDL levels. This is because carbohydrates increase cholesterol production in the liver. A high-carbohydrate diet causes more fat deposits in muscles, blood vessels, and adipose tissues. Eventually, excess fat forms deposits on artery walls. This affects the circulatory system.

Low LDL levels are desirable in maintaining good health. While exercise helps to reduce LDL levels, a restricted low-fat diet is better. To reduce LDL levels, one should eat fruits, vegetables, whole grains, and beans. One should avoid fatty foods like red meat and whole-milk dairy products. One should also avoid low-fat, low-fiber foods like bread, pasta, pastries, and cookies. Finally, one should eat five or more small meals per day rather than three large meals. It slows down the liver's production of insulin (sugar) and cholesterol.

> **Item:** LDL level
> **Points (Primary Details):** bad cholesterol; high-carbohydrate diet; excess fat; affects circulation
> **Word Clues:** *first, bad, raises, low, reduce, finally*

The second component is HDL (high-density lipoproteins). This is considered good cholesterol. Produced within the liver, HDL contains substances that do not bind to cell membranes. Instead it carries surplus cholesterol back to the liver. There it gets recycled or excreted. Thus, high levels of HDL prevent fat deposits in blood vessels. This leads to a lower risk of heart disease.

High HDL levels are desirable. They can be improved by aerobic exercise at least four days per week for at least 30 minutes per session. A healthy diet is also important in maintaining high HDL levels. High levels of HDL are considered a negative risk factor for heart disease and seem to predict vascular health.

> **Item:** HDL level
> **Points (Primary Details):** good cholesterol; negative factor for heart disease
> **Word Clues:** *second, good, desirable, high*

Read the following passage to determine what items are being compared. Then note the points within the comparison. List these three points as broadly as possible, creating primary details. List one supporting detail for each point. You may find it helpful to underline the word clues in each paragraph.

Dog lovers prize the elegant miniature poodle as a pampered house dog. This small dog, also called the French poodle, came from Europe in the 1500s. Its name, poodle, came from the German word *pfundel,* or "splash." The miniature poodle descended from water dogs of Germany and Russia. However, it also is linked to France, where it was known as the *caniche*. This name referred to its superb duck-hunting skill. The miniature poodle became popular with the French aristocracy. It was named the national dog of France.

The miniature poodle is a member of the nonsporting group of pure-bred dogs. It is an active, intelligent animal, usually 15 inches tall or less. It is an elegant dog. However, it can be trained easily. It also makes an excellent watchdog. The miniature poodle has curly, dense hair. Its coat may be solid blue, gray, brown, apricot, or cream colored. It always has dark eyes.

On the other hand, dog lovers also prize the robust Siberian husky. This dog comes from a hardy, outdoor breed. This furry dog came from northeastern Siberia. It was trained by the Chukchi people as a sled dog. In 1909, a large number of these "Chukchi dogs" were brought to Alaska to compete in the dog races. During the winter of 1925, the Siberian huskies became famous when they carried needed serum to the isolated town of Nome, Alaska. By 1930, the Siberian husky had become established as a breed.

The Siberian husky is a member of the working group of dogs. This medium-sized, 45–60-pound animal is bred for pulling sleds. Affectionate and intelligent, it is quick and light on its feet. However, it is not easily trained. A strong and durable dog, the Siberian husky has a soft, dense undercoat of hair that supports an outer coat. The outer coat may range in color from white to black. Its eyes may be brown or blue.

Items: _____

Points (Primary Details): _____

_____

Supporting Details (Minor Details): _____

_____

Using a Graphic Organizer

You can use a graphic organizer like the one that follows to prepare for making an outline. In the center box, briefly describe the purpose for the comparison. List one item being compared on the top of the Item #1 box. Then, inside the box, fill in the points of comparison. Add supporting details under each point. Do the same for the remaining boxes as needed. After you have finished, the organizer should give you a clear overview of the comparison/contrast pattern in your reading passage.

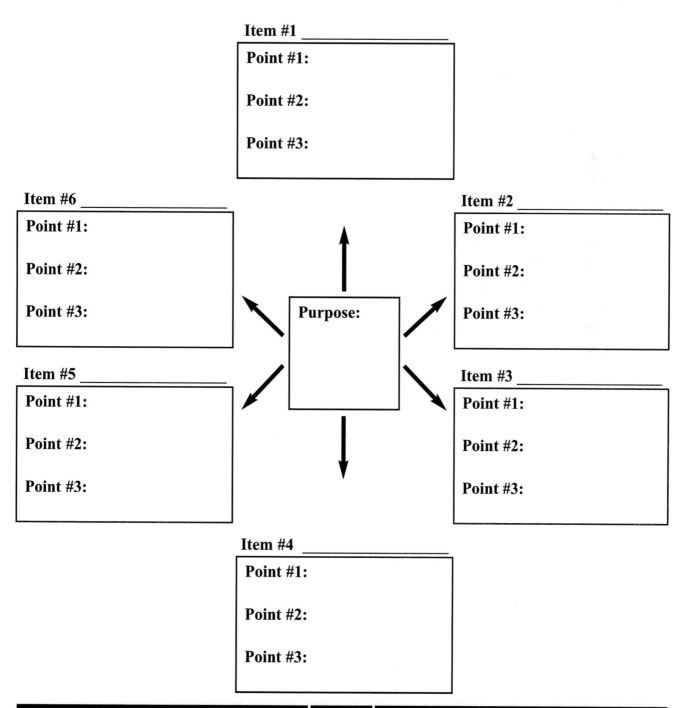

Designing the Comparison/Contrast Pattern Outline

If two items are being compared, each item should have a Roman-numeral heading. Each point of comparison is a capital-letter entry under its corresponding item. The points should be the same for each item being compared. They should be in the same order. Supporting details should go under their related points with Arabic-number entries. As always, the outline moves from general to specific as the entries move from left to right. Look back at Activity 26. It compares the miniature poodle with the Siberian husky. Here is what the start of an outline based on that reading might look like:

Two Different Dogs
    I. The miniature poodle
      A. History
         1. Water dog from Germany, Russia, France (1500s)
         2. Became national dog of France
      B. Characteristics
         1. Nonsporting dog
         2. Easily trained
    II. The Siberian husky
      A. History
         1. From NE Siberia
         2. Trained as a sled dog in Alaska (1900s)
      B. Characteristics
         1. Working dog
         2. Not easily trained

If more than two items are being compared, the purpose for the comparison is given the first Roman-numeral heading. The general description of the items are then given the second Roman-numeral heading. Each individual item being compared is a capital-letter entry under the item title. Next, each point of comparison is an Arabic-numeral entry under each capital letter. The points should be the same for each item, and they should be in the same order. Finally, supporting details are lowercase-letter entries. As always, the outline moves from general to specific as the entries move from left to right. Look back at Activity 24. It compares several ice cream flavors to personality types. Here is what the start of an outline based on that reading might look like:

Know Yourself by Your Flavor
    I. Linking personality to ice cream flavors
    II. Ice cream flavors
        A. Vanilla
            1. Enjoys close family relations
                a. Impulsive
                b. Risk-taker
            2. Gets along only with vanilla lovers
        B. Chocolate
            1. Enjoys being center of attention
                a. Lively
                b. Creative
            2. Gets along with butter-pecan/chocolate-chip lovers
    etc.

Building a Comparison/Contrast Outline

Building a comparison/contrast outline involves combining the steps you have learned in this chapter. You may want to use the graphic organizer to record the information you gather. When the organizer is completed, use it to fill in your outline.

If two items are being compared:

1. List each item as a Roman-numeral entry.

2. Determine the points of comparison. Make sure they are the same points for each item. Place the points under each item in the same order. List each point as a capital-letter entry.

3. When there are supporting details, list at least two under the related point. They should be Arabic-numeral entries. You may not need many supporting details in your outline.

4. Finally, title the outline. Try to capture both the comparison and the author's viewpoint.

If more than two items are being compared:

1. Determine the purpose of the comparison. Write the purpose as the first Roman-numeral heading. Write the general description of the items being compared as the second Roman-numeral heading.

2. List each item being compared as a capital-letter entry.

3. Determine the points of comparison. Make sure they are the same points for each item. Place them under each item in the same order. List each point as an Arabic-numeral entry.

4. When there are supporting details, list at least two under the related point. Give them lowercase-letter entries. You may not need many supporting details in your outline.

5. Finally, title the outline. Try to capture both the comparison and the author's viewpoint.

Following the steps listed on page 76, make a short outline for the next reading. Do not use more than two Roman-numeral headings.

Dear Mom,

I am having an awful time rooming here. My roommate and I can't seem to get along. Dorm life is getting to be a real hassle. I think my roommate is an okay person, but we have different habits.

I know I'm a slob, but man, I never saw anyone who was so picky. I leave my stuff around, and she's always putting her things away. She's a neat freak.

I'm probably too noisy for her. I like to listen to music while I study, and I like to talk on the phone. She wants it quiet so she can concentrate when she studies.

I stay up past midnight, and she goes to bed at 10. But then she gets up early to study. She always wakes me up getting up and moving around. Sometimes she turns on the light and watches television.

We started out okay, but now we are barely speaking. What do I do?

Love,
Anna

Outline Title: _____

   I. _____

      A. _____

      B. _____

         1. _____

         2. _____

      C. _____

  II. _____

      A. _____

      B. _____

      C. _____

         1. _____

         2. _____

Here is a longer reading to practice on. Follow the same steps as you did in Activity 27. However, this time make your own outline on a separate sheet of paper. Use no more than two Roman-numeral headings. Remember, proper outline style means that you should not have just one capital-letter entry and/or Arabic-numeral entry. You must have at least two.

Candy is a favorite American treat. It entices anyone who loves sweets. Candies can spoil appetites and increase body weight. Yet, many shoppers buy candy anyway.

Candy originates from our past. The concept of eating a sweet treat is not a recent practice. Early humans at honey from beehives. Later, the Egyptians, Arabs, and Chinese prepared confections of fruit, nuts, and honey. People in the Middle Ages ate sweets made out of sugar until the cost of sugar made sweets scarce. In England and later in the American colonies, people ate boiled sugar candies. During the early nineteenth century, candy was made from boiling water at various stages. Hard candies, lemon drops, and peppermints became popular and later were mass-produced. Since then, a variety of non-chocolate candies appeared on the market. Types of non-chocolate candies now include hard candy, sugar-coated candy, chewy candy, jelly candy, peppermint candy, tart candy, gum, and mints.

In contrast to the Old World history of non-chocolate candies, the story of chocolate candy began in the New World. In 1492, Columbus arrived in the Americas and learned about the cocoa bean. He learned that the natives used it in a drink.

Later, the cocoa bean was transformed into a confection. In 1847, "eating chocolate" became fondant chocolate. Milk chocolate was produced, ushering in chocolate candy. In 1868, Valentine boxes of chocolates were introduced by Richard Cadbury. In 1900, the milk-chocolate bar was marketed by Milton Hershey. Over the next 70 years, a variety of chocolate confections continued to tantalize the American public. Types of chocolate candy now include cookie bars and ice-cream bars. Americans love sweets, but most Americans prefer chocolate. Chocolate in all its variety has become a part of American culture: our curse, yet our delight!

Recognizing the Pattern

The general statement followed by specific examples is an easy pattern to recognize. Once you spot the general statement, the specific examples are not hard to find. Sometimes the general statement is stated clearly within the first sentence or paragraph. Other times, the general statement may be stated indirectly or implied. In either case, you may need to restate the central theme in order to form a simple general statement. Paraphrasing or summarizing is an easy way to restate the central theme.

This two-part pattern occurs in feature articles with general information. In school, the **general/specific** pattern appears in social studies, science, and literature textbooks. It may also be in readings for psychology, technology, driver's education, art, and music classes.

In both examples below, the general statement is stated clearly in the first sentence. Note that in both examples, the first sentence is also the central theme running throughout the selection. Both examples reflect the general/specific pattern in which the general statement is backed up by a list of related things or ideas that serve as examples. These examples, or major items, may appear in sequential order. They may also appear in order of importance.

Example 1 (Sequential order)
The weekend is the highlight of the week. On Friday night, many people go out to the movies. Or they go out to eat or just hang out with friends. On Saturday morning, many people sleep later than usual. Then they spend the day doing chores or running errands. Some attend sporting events or religious services. On Sunday, the most relaxed day of the week, many people entertain family and friends. They may go to entertainment attractions and performances. Or they go to sports practices and games. Many attend church services.

Example 2 (Order of importance)
The weekend is the favorite part of the week for many people. First, they relish the time to relax. Second, they delight in not having to follow a set schedule. Finally, they enjoy staying up on Friday and Saturday nights and sleeping in on Saturday and Sunday mornings.

Example 3 is a longer selection. The general statement appears as a central theme in the introduction. The supporting major items are presented in the body. The general statement is restated in the conclusion. At the end of the reading, note that the general statement has been rephrased in order to state the central theme more simply.

Example 3
Introduction
Summer is the most relaxing season of the year. Students are free from the regimen of classes. For most, a comfortable summer schedule provides needed change from school demands.

Body
June is the most carefree month of the summer. Students quickly become used to not following a routine. They readily adapt to a relaxed schedule. They relish staying up to watch movies, play games, or just hang around with friends instead of having to go to bed early. Waking up late and lounging around the house is much more pleasant than having to hustle off to school. No matter what the activity, students will not be bored in June. To them, only school is boring; being out of school is great. Any activity—baseball, swimming, camp, even work—gets a positive response. However, after a few weeks, boredom begins to set in.

July is not as interesting as June. July's heat limits outdoor activities. Consequently, students become homebound. Being "off" from school begins to lose its punch. After the Fourth of July, students begin to grow tired of watching television and playing games. When organized sports end, many students become more irritable. Because bored students need a change of scene, July is an excellent time for planning family vacations and outings.

By August, most students silently long for the return to a more structured routine. They have played out their distaste for a structured regimen. Now they begin to focus on school friends and activities. Athletes anticipate being on soccer, cross-country, and football teams. Cheerleaders and band members look forward to performing at games. They are not enthusiastic about going to classes and having to study. Yet, most students will admit grudgingly that they are ready for school to start. As the first days of school near, students begin to anticipate a different schedule.

Conclusion
Changes in routine during the summer help students have good attitudes toward their structured school schedules. Rest and relaxation give students energy for another school year.

> **General Statement:** Summer vacation gives students a relaxing break from demanding school schedules.

Characteristics of the General/Specific Pattern

In the general/specific pattern, the general statement and supporting examples (major items) often show a whole/part relationship. For this to work, the examples must be similar. Look at **Example 1.** Notice the word *weekend* in the first sentence. This is the "whole." Now look at the "parts": the days *Friday, Saturday,* and *Sunday* in the following sentences. Look at **Example 3.** What word in the first sentence shows the whole? What words in the second, third, and fourth paragraphs show the parts?

A "category" noun in the first sentence also may introduce the major items that will follow. Some category words are *character, citation, figure, history, model, pattern, sample,* and *tips.* Verbs such as *characterize, demonstrate, exemplify, indicate, model, portray,* and *show* also may signal examples (major items) to follow.

Major items may be introduced with ordering words such as *first, second, next,* or *finally.* Look at **Example 1** again. There are no ordering words. When do you think ordering words are needed?

If a reading contains a general statement supported by similar examples, listed either in sequence or in order of importance, it is probably in general/specific pattern.

The passage in **Example 4** describes two Norse gods. We can recognize it as a general/specific pattern because of the whole/part relationship shown. The "whole" is the phrase *Norse gods.* Individual gods are the examples, or major items. Note the ordering words that introduce both examples. Note that the general statement is restated as the central theme linking both examples.

Example 4

Norse gods mirror the fierce spirit of the Vikings. The first example is Odin, the primary god. He was king of the gods in Norse mythology. His greatest treasures were his 8-foot steed, Sleipner; his spear, Gunger; and his ring, Draupner. As god of war, Odin held court in Valhalla. This was where all brave warriors went after death in battle. He had two black ravens, Huginn (Thought) and Muninn (Memory). They flew forth to gather news for Odin. Odin was also the god of wisdom, poetry, and magic. He sacrificed an eye for the privilege of drinking from Mimir. This was the fountain of wisdom.

The second example is Thor, the most fearsome of the Norse gods. In Norse mythology, Thor was the god of thunder. He was the strongest of the Aesir, the chief gods. He helped protect the Aesir from their enemies, the giants. Thor had a magic hammer, which he threw with iron gloves. The hammer always returned to him. Thursday is named for Thor.

> **General Statement:** Norse gods show the fierce Viking spirit.
> **Major Items:** Odin, god of war; Thor, god of thunder

General/Specific Pattern

Once you identify the general/specific pattern in your reading, these strategies can help you read and understand the material:

1. Read the first paragraph, or the introductory paragraphs, carefully. Find the general statement. Skim the rest of the paragraphs to find the supporting examples (major items). Then read the concluding paragraph. Figure out whether the theme of the general statement continues through the whole selection.

2. As you read the first and last paragraphs, note the general statement and the main idea. See if the main idea reflects the author's opinion. Look for adjectives and adverbs that convey the author's viewpoint. Note how the title reflects the main idea.

3. Read the selection carefully. Find the supporting examples. Look for category nouns that may label these major items. Look for whole/part relationships that identify major items. Look for verbs that may signal these.

4. Look for ordering words like *first, second, next,* and *finally*. They may introduce supporting examples, or major items. (These can also be called primary details.) Also identify the key details (secondary details) that correspond to major items.

5. Reread the selection. Mentally note or rephrase the general statement. Note the main idea, the author's viewpoint, the major items, and the title.

Use the reading strategies listed on page 82 to read the next passage. Then write the general statement on the line that follows. Look for the category word in the first sentence. Then write four supporting major items on the lines provided.

North Dakota is a bountiful state with diverse natural resources. Large petroleum deposits can be found in western North Dakota in the Williston Basin. Also, one of the largest lignite reserves in the nation sits in western North Dakota. Throughout the state, sand and gravel are mined from the natural rock. Finally, gas is produced from the earth. North Dakota's resources distinguish this unique northern state.

General Statement: _____

Category Word: _____

Major Items: _____

_____

_____

_____

Now try applying this approach to a longer selection. Using your reading strategies, read the selection carefully. On the lines that follow, write the general statement. List the descriptive words in the first paragraph that show the author's viewpoint. Then list the major items that support the general statement.

Ice cream, with its smooth, sweet taste, is one of America's favorite desserts. Nothing can compare with a dish of delicious ice cream, particularly on a hot summer day.

The history of ice cream is a long one. It began in the fourth century B.C.E. This was when the Emperor Nero ordered ice combined with fruit. Later, in the thirteenth century, Marco Polo brought back Chinese milk-and-ice concoctions to Europe. Over time, recipes for ices and sherbets were created and served in the French and Italian royal courts. Ice cream was introduced in England during the seventeenth century. It came to America during the eighteenth century.

During the nineteenth century, several innovations brought about the manufacture of ice cream. In 1846, Nancy Johnson of New Jersey invented the first portable hand-cranked ice cream freezer. In 1851, Jacob Fussell, a Baltimore milk dealer, started the first wholesale ice cream business. Salt and ice were used to lower and control the temperature of the ice cream mix. Then the wooden bucket freezer with rotary paddles was invented. This increased production.

The twentieth century added more variety to ice cream. In 1904, at the St. Louis World Fair, Ernest A. Hamwi, a Syrian pastry maker, introduced the pastry cone. Charles E. Minches thought of filling these cones with two scoops of ice cream. Later, many exotic flavors began appearing. New brands of ice cream flooded the supermarkets. Ice cream franchises marketed new concoctions. Today, ice cream continues to be a favorite treat!

General Statement: _____

Descriptors: _____

Major Items: _____

_____

_____

_____

The Main Idea

The main idea in the general/specific pattern is the central idea or theme behind the general statement and its specific examples. The main idea is the author's view or "take" on the general statement. For example, in Activity 30, the descriptor *delicious* shows the author's liking for ice cream. Later in the selection, the general statement is made (*the history of ice cream is a long one*). This leads to the main idea—the popularity of ice cream over many centuries.

Sometimes you can find a clear idea of the author's viewpoint in the first paragraph. At other times, you will need to look further. Note the author's use of descriptive words. These include adjectives and adverbs, but other word choices can tell you a lot. Does the author explain the general statement? How does the author end the general statement?

Understanding the author's opinion will help you in several ways. If you can tell the author's viewpoint, you can weigh it for bias. You can use it to identify the main idea. And you can use it later when you need a title for your outline.

At times, the author tries to maintain a neutral stance. No descriptors give away the author's viewpoint. In these cases, the general statement simply becomes the main idea.

Read the selection in **Example 5.** Note the author's viewpoint in the use of descriptors.

Example 5

Crayola™ crayons have won the praise of children throughout the world. The first crayons, a mixture of charcoal and oil, began in Europe. In the early 1900s, an American chemical company, Binney & Smith, developed a wax crayon. It was similar to one they used to mark crates and boxes. Their brand name, Crayola, combined the French word for "chalk," *craie*, with *ola*, a variation of "oily."

In 1903, Crayola crayons were introduced to the American public. The original Crayolas were a boxed set of eight colors: black, blue, brown, green, orange, red, violet, and yellow. Between 1949 and 1957, 40 new colors were introduced. These colors included apricot and carnation pink. Between 1972 and 1989, fluorescent colors were added. Currently, there are 120 colors. This wide variety of hues stimulates creativity in children.

Today, Crayolas continue to be popular items. Children love them. Parents love Crayolas, too. The crayons bring back happy memories of their own art projects.

> **Descriptors:** *praise, popular, happy*
> **Viewpoint:** Crayola crayons spark creativity, and they are popular with all ages.

Read the next selection. Look for the main idea. On the lines below the passage, write the general statement, key descriptors, and the main idea.

Many ancient winter holiday traditions arose in the dark, cold Scandinavian countries. These celebrations emphasized warmth and light. One old tradition was the burning of the Yule log. Originally, the Yule log was an entire tree. It was brought into the house with great fanfare. The root end of the tree was placed in the hearth, and the tree was burned throughout the celebration. Today, the Yule log is only referred to in Christmas carols. In some Scandinavian countries, however, a Yule candle is still burned.

Another tradition revolves around the use of candles during the Christmas season. In Sweden, candles are burned on St. Lucia's Day. This tradition dates back to the fourth century. Modern Swedes still launch the Christmas season by celebrating St. Lucia's Day on December 13. According to custom, the eldest daughter wears a wreath of seven lighted candles on her head. She serves coffee and buns to every family member.

General Statement: _____

Descriptors: _____

Main Idea: _____

Titling the Reading: A Guide to the Main Idea

If a reading selection does not have a title, it is helpful to create one. It can help you identify the main idea. It will also help later when you need to give your outline a title. The title should reflect both the general statement and the author's viewpoint. Try to keep it short—no more than five words. **Example 6** describes how Kwanza is celebrated. Descriptive words tell how the author views Kwanza.

Example 6

The week of Kwanza is celebrated between December 26 and January 1. It provides a festive opportunity to celebrate seven traditional African values. These revolve around self-responsibility, self-improvement, family togetherness, community, and commerce. During this enjoyable celebration week, one value is honored on each day. On December 31, the final feast of Kwanza, or Karumu, is held. The Karumu is a meaningful, communal feast. It recognizes community as a traditional African value.

The Kwanza celebration ends with the exchange of gifts. Although this can occur throughout the week of Kwanza, presents are traditionally given on January 1. Gifts exchanged between parents and children are often educational or artistic.

The adjectives *festive, enjoyable,* and *meaningful* show the author's opinion about Kwanza. A title such as "The Importance of Kwanza" reflects the author's viewpoint.

Titling Strategies

Sometimes it is easy to think of a title for a reading. At other times, you may need to use a system. If you cannot think of a title, try "building" one by following these steps:

1. Identify the general statement and main idea.

2. Find the descriptive words that illustrate the general statement or main idea.

3. Restate the general statement or main idea. Incorporate key descriptors.

4. If you cannot think of a title that sums up the general statement, use a generic title. The general statement can be covered by a collective noun, such as *Examples of* _____ or *History of* _____ .

5. Limit your title to five words.

Read the passage below. Identify the general statement. Look for descriptors that show the author's viewpoint or bias. Then create a title for the selection. On the lines below the reading, write the general statement, key descriptors, and title.

Three modern Christmas traditions are rooted in ancient beliefs and customs. In fact, they date back over a thousand years. The first tradition is the 12 days of Christmas. It relates to the ancient Mesopotamian god Marduk, who was thought to battle with the monsters of chaos each year. To help him, the ancient Mesopotamians held a New Year festival. This was called Zagmuk, and it lasted for 12 days. The second tradition is the use of evergreen in festive decorations. This can be traced to the Druids, who saw the evergreen as a symbol of everlasting life. It can also be traced to the Vikings, who viewed the evergreen as a special plant of their sun god, Balden. Later, the Romans used evergreen trees and candles to decorate their homes during Saturnalia. This was a major Roman festival. In fact, the final tradition—the exchange of gifts—can be linked to Saturnalia. This ancient holiday celebrating the Roman gods was later banned by the church. However, gift-giving has lasted through the centuries as part of the modern Christmas celebration.

General Statement: _____

Descriptors: _____

Title: _____

Recognizing the Major Items

The general/specific pattern in longer selections is usually made up of major items (primary details) and major details (secondary details). Sometimes a major detail contains an additional supporting detail or minor detail. This can be confusing. You need to distinguish between each major item and the major detail that supports it.

The example below presents some tips for dealing with stress. Each tip is a major item. Each item has some supporting details (major details). Your job is to sort out the details so that you can remember the tips. By doing so, you will be identifying the building blocks of the general/specific pattern: the major items.

Example 7

Stress affects our health. Positively, stress can cause new responses and achievements. Negatively, it can create stress symptoms: anger, rejection, distrust, and depression. These feelings can lead to further health problems like upset stomach, rashes, headache, stroke, or heart attack. Keeping a positive attitude while dealing with stress is an important skill.

First, recognize the stressors in your life. Reduce them as much as possible. If you can, eliminate them. Start saying "no" to requests that you will find stressful.

> **Major Item (Primary Detail):** reduce/eliminate stressors
> **Major Details:** recognize stressors; say "no" to stressful requests

Second, if you cannot eliminate stressors in your life, limit your contact time with them. Avoid them. Or reduce your exposure to unavoidable stressors. Try taking a break or leaving the area where you feel the stress.

> **Major Item (Primary Detail):** avoid stressors
> **Major Details:** take break; leave stressful area

Finally, don't sweat the small stuff, and don't lose your temper. Before you get angry, put things in perspective. Not every circumstance is as critical or urgent as you think. Try not to react to negatives quickly. Count to 10 or to 100 before you respond verbally. Try deep-breathing techniques to lower your heart rate. Overreacting makes an emotionally-charged situation worse, when it needs defusing. Calm, collected behavior produces better results.

> **Major Item (Primary Detail):** don't lose your temper
> **Major Details:** put things in perspective; try counting or deep-breathing; don't overreact; be calm

Unlike shorter readings, longer general/specific passages may be more difficult. Often, you may have to combine major details and rename several details as one major item. Of course, you should still keep track of the major details relating to each item. These will be the supporting details in your outline.

The example below describes tips for skin care. While you read, notice how the tips are made from supporting details. Also note how supporting details can be combined and renamed.

Example 8

Regardless of age, most people would like softer, younger-looking skin. A radiant complexion is a mark of beauty and a measure of health for both men and women. So, sensible skin care is important. Here are some tips on how to make your skin look young and vibrant.

Daily, your skin endures its environment. This means grease, grime, germs, oils, sweat, cosmetics, and pollutants. At one time, many people believed that scrubbing their skin with strong soap and hot water cleaned their skin. Today, more people use special skin cleansers. They irritate the skin less than conventional soaps. They also leave fewer residues. Dermatologists recommend gentleness, especially when washing the face.

> **Major Item (Primary Detail):** cleaning the skin
> **Major Details:** use of skin cleansers; gentleness

As you age, the glands in your skin produce less oil. The result is dry skin. Dryness causes wrinkling. Moisturizers should be used to smooth dry skin. Moisturizers lock water into the skin while drawing water from the skin's lower layers.

> **Major Item (Primary Detail):** moisturizing the skin
> **Major Details:** decrease in skin oils; use of moisturizers

Sun exposure causes most skin damage. This includes roughening, wrinkling, discoloration, broken blood vessels, sallowness, sagging, and skin cancers. Skin should always be protected from the sun. There is no such thing as a healthy tan. Skin damage caused by overexposure to the sun may take 20 years to show, but it is definitely a skin-aging factor.

> **Major Item (Primary Detail):** protecting skin from sun
> **Major Details:** types of skin damage; no healthy tan; skin-aging factor

Word Clues

Ordering words such as *first, second, next, also,* and *finally* can help you recognize major items in the general/specific pattern. Look for whole/part relationships between the general statement and supporting major items. Category nouns like *character, citation, figure, history, model, pattern, sample,* and *tips* rename major items. They provide additional clues. Finally, verbs such as *characterize, demonstrate, exemplify, indicate, model, portray,* and *show* signal the general/specific pattern.

Read the selection below carefully. Note the word clues that identify each major item.

Example 9

Wouldn't it be wonderful if money really did grow on trees? If you needed it, you could just pick as much money as you wanted. No stress, no worries—but no motivation.

Being wealthy isn't something that just happens. Most Americans are not rich from inheriting wealth or winning the lottery. Rather, most Americans become wealthy because they work hard and practice good money management. Saving money over a lifetime does not sound very exciting. However, savings produce wealth.

How do you save? First, start early. Don't wait to save, because time is important. Losing a chance to save means loss of potential investments and profits. Instead, save consistently. Set aside an amount you have chosen to save every month and save it. Don't be sidetracked. You will always have monthly bills, but still you should save.

> **Major Item (Primary Detail):** save early and consistently
> **Major Details:** time is important in wealth accumulation; save the same amount every month
> **Word Clue:** *first*

Then, do not spend more than you make. Going into debt will keep you from saving. Instead, know how you spend money. Itemize your expenses. Be aware of where your money goes. Keep track of your credit card and credit card expenses. Pay off your creditors as soon as possible.

> **Major Item (Primary Detail):** control spending
> **Major Details:** do not go into debt; itemize your expenses; keep track of how you spend your money; pay off your credit cards
> **Word Clues:** *then*

Read the following selection. Identify the general statement, major items, and supporting major details. Rename the major items as broadly as possible, creating primary details. Look for word clues in the reading. Finally, write down the major details, major items, and the general statement on the lines provided.

Water polo is an unusual sport that is growing in popularity. But, to fully appreciate this attractive sport, one must understand how the game is played.

Each team has 12 members. Only seven members—six offensive players and a defensive goalie—can play at one time, though. The six field players are all offensive drivers. They move the ball toward the goal while trying to pass or shoot the ball. The point man is the top center driver, farthest away from the goal. Two flats, flanking the top center driver's left and right, are closer to the goal. The hole man is the offensive player placed anywhere inside the penalty throw zone. The hole man also plays defense, guarding the goal. Two wings flank the hole man on the right and left. The seventh player, the defensive goalie, guards the goal.

Major Item (Primary Detail): _____

Major Details: _____

Rules govern the passage of the ball. One important rule is that the ball only can be handled by one hand. If a player uses both hands to pass the ball, the referee will call a turnover. The ball goes to the opposing team. Also, lines on the pool deck mark specific regions in which special rules of play must be observed. For example, the 2-meter line is drawn from goalposts on both sides of the pool. It prohibits offensive players from entering without possessing the ball. If offensive players enter this prohibited area without the ball, a turnover is called. The 4-meter line marks the location from which penalty shots on the goal may be taken. Penalty shots are given to an offensive player who is fouled within the 4-meter line while trying to score.

Although the rules of play and level of competition may vary, men usually play four seven-minute quarters. Women play four six-minute quarters. Teams are allowed two timeouts per game.

Major Item (Primary Detail): _____

Major Details: _____

General Statement: _____

Using a Graphic Organizer

You can use a graphic organizer like this one to prepare for making an outline. Briefly write the general statement in the general statement box. Then write the first major item in the appropriate box. Write each major detail under the first major item. Do the same thing for the remaining major items. If there are more than two major items, title them. Use a noun that renames the major items, or use a word like *examples, procedures, samples,* or *steps* in your title.

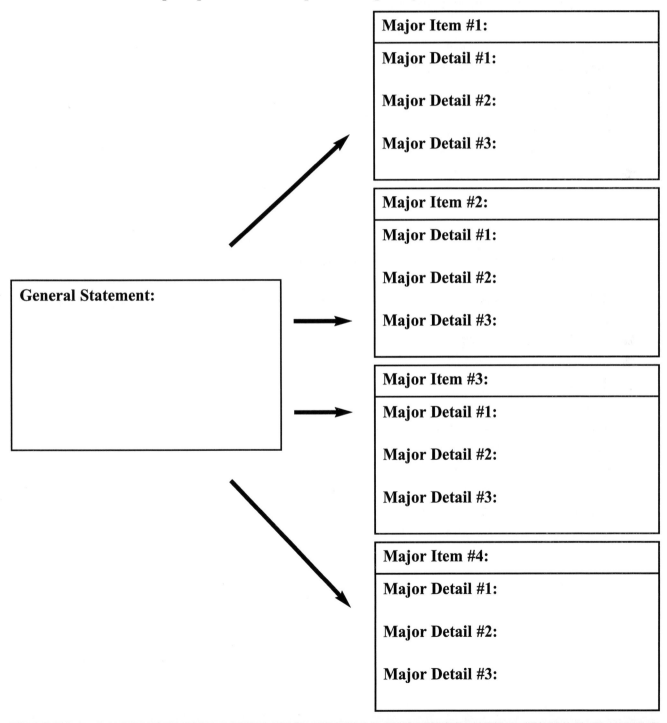

Designing the General/Specific Pattern Outline

In a general/specific outline, the general statement should be titled and given the first Roman-numeral heading. The major items are then titled in the second Roman-numeral heading. Each individual major item is a capital-letter entry. Major details are listed as Arabic-numeral entries under the related capital-letter entries. As always, the outline moves from general to specific as the entries move from left to right. Look back at **Example 8.** It tells how to care for your skin. Here is what an outline based on that example might look like:

Tips for Younger-Looking Skin
    I. The importance of sensible skin care
    II. Procedures
        A. Cleaning
            1. Facial cleansers
            2. Gentle washing
        B. Moisturizing
        C. Protecting

In outlines with only two major items, the general statement may be covered in the title. Each major item has a Roman-numeral heading. Major details should be listed under their major item as capital-letter entries. Minor details are listed under these as Arabic-numeral entries. Look back at **Example 4.** It describes two Norse gods. Here is what an outline based on that example might look like:

Ferocious Viking Gods
    I. Odin
        A. Primary god
        B. God of war, wisdom, poetry, magic
    II. Thor
        A. God of thunder
            1. Most fearsome of Norse gods
            2. Strongest of chief gods
        B. Thursday named for Thor

Building a General/Specific Outline

Building a general/specific outline involves combining the steps you have learned in this chapter. You may want to use the graphic organizer to record the information you gather. When the organizer is completed, use it to fill in your outline.

If more than two major items are involved:

1. Identify the general statement and the supporting major items. Title the general statement and give it the first Roman-numeral heading. Title the major items. Give this title the second Roman-numeral heading.

2. Identify the major items. List each major item as a capital-letter entry.

3. If there are major details, list at least two under the related capital-letter entry. These should be Arabic-numeral entries.

4. Finally, title the outline. Try to capture both the general statement and the author's viewpoint.

If only two major items are involved:

1. Identify the general statement. Look for the author's viewpoint. Include both within your title.

2. Identify the major items. List each item as a Roman-numeral heading.

3. List at least two major details under each Roman-numeral heading. These should be capital-letter entries.

4. If major details are supported by minor details, list at least two minor details under the related capital-letter entry. These should be Arabic-numeral entries.

Create a short outline for the next selection. Follow the steps listed on page 95. Do not use more than two Roman-numeral headings.

Chocolate ranks as a favorite snack among Americans. Yet, many Americans feel guilty about eating chocolate. Why? Perhaps because chocolate is misrepresented as a luxury food linked to obesity. High in fat and carbohydrates, chocolate is often wrongly associated with weight gain and eating disorders. However, chocolate itself does not cause eating binges. When eaten in moderation, chocolate is actually a nutritious food. It is rich in potassium and magnesium.

Many people wrongly associate chocolate with acne. In reality, test studies have not linked the eating of chocolate with a significant change in acne. Yet, many Americans deprive themselves of chocolate in order to maintain a clear complexion.

Many people also think there is a high caffeine level in chocolate. However, the actual amount of caffeine in chocolate is very low. A 1.4-ounce piece of milk chocolate contains the same amount of caffeine as a cup of decaffeinated coffee.

Others associate chocolate with allergies. A small number of people may react to chocolate products. However, allergies to chocolate often occur in confectionary plants. Workers have developed allergies to the cocoa bean and to chocolate products being processed. Moreover, children who are allergic to chocolate often outgrow the allergy.

Let's set the record straight. Chocolate is not a health hazard. Americans should get over their hangups and should savor chocolate! Chocolate is food for the gods. It should be given its special place in our diets—of course, in moderation.

Outline Title: _____

    I. _____

   II. _____

       A. _____

          1._____

          2._____

       B. _____

       C. _____

       D. _____

Here is a longer reading. Follow the same steps as you did for Activity 34. This time, though, create your own outline on a separate sheet of paper. Use no more than two Roman-numeral headings. Remember, proper outline style means that you should not have just one capital-letter and/or Arabic-numeral entry. You must have at least two.

Do you wish to become wealthy? Then you must begin setting your goals accordingly. Once you are out of debt, manage your money and start saving. The first place to invest is in a home. Owning your own home is your most important lifetime investment. Its value depends upon the square footage, location, and overall condition.

Another investment option is a savings account. Saving accounts are good places to store emergency cash. They are insured by the FDIC for up to $100,000. They also are easily accessible. However, the interest rate on savings accounts is low. Money market accounts earn slightly higher interest rates. They are also accessible to the investor. However, they may require an initial deposit of a thousand dollars. Withdrawal may be limited, too.

Certificates of deposit (CDs) earn more interest and are a low-risk investment. This is because the FDIC also insures CDs for up to $100,000. However, access is limited in that the money is invested for a fixed period of time. The longer the period, the greater the interest on the money you invest.

401(k) plans are good plans aimed at retirement savings. Under these plans, you can contribute a certain percentage of your gross income. This reduces your current income tax rate. Also, some employers contribute matching funds to the 401(k) plan. This adds to its worth. Over a period of time, the accrued savings grow within the plan. All 401(k) monies are tax-deferred until the money is withdrawn. At that time, income tax on the accrued savings must be paid. Money may not be withdrawn without a penalty until you are 59½. If you do take out money beforehand, a 20% withholding fee is required. There is also a 10% IRS penalty fee. However, investment options exist for the 401(k) plan. You may choose from stock, bond, and mutual-fund options that fluctuate with market rates.

Stocks are another type of investment that depends on market conditions. If a company does well, investors get dividends or can sell at a profit. If the company does poorly, they may lose their investment. Bonds are considered a safer investment than stocks. A bond certificate guarantees a specific interest rate at a fixed rate of income. It may be sold before it matures, but then it is subject to interest fluctuations. Thus, if interest rates rise before the maturation date, the bond may lose its face value. Whatever your investment, saving money to earn more money is a smart move.

Recognizing the Pattern

A special term and its definition is another common pattern to see in reading selections. You can find this two-part pattern in articles that introduce an object or idea. In school, the **definitive pattern** is often found in science textbooks. It also appears in readings for social studies, literature, psychology, art, and music classes.

In the definitive pattern, the term is first presented. Then it is defined. The definition may be presented in sequence. Or the definition may show a whole/part relationship between sentences. Here are two simple examples of the definitive pattern.

> **Example 1 (Definition in sequential sentences)**
> The elephant is an interesting animal related to the mastodon and the mammoth. *First*, the elephant is huge, weighing 11,000 to 15,000 pounds. *Second*, elephants feature unique ivory tusks and flexible trunks. *Finally*, elephants exist in two varieties. Smaller-eared elephants inhabit Asia, while larger-eared elephants occupy Africa.

> **Example 2 (Definition in whole/part sentences)**
> The kangaroo is a unique Australian marsupial. Its large, sheeplike *head* has big, moveable *ears*. Its slender *chest* has a *pouch* in which the kangaroo carries its young. Its short front *legs*, powerful back *legs,* and long, muscular *tail* provide unusual motion and balance to this amazing animal.

Characteristics of the Definitive Pattern

In longer definitive readings, the defined term is presented in the introduction along with the main idea. Then the term is further defined in one or more sections. The definition is supported by all the sections. Each section expands the term in a different way. A section may explain the term, cite characteristics or habits, or give examples. It may give its history, illustrate the term, or give uses for the term. A section may compare the term to another term, cite a process related to the term, cite causes and/or effects relating to it, or cite problems/solutions related to it. Finally, the conclusion sums up the significance of the term and the main idea.

In the example on the next page, the cheetah is defined briefly in the introduction. In the second paragraph, its body characteristics are listed as the first section. In the third paragraph, its hunting habits are described as the second section.

Example 3
Introduction
The cheetah is an endangered member of the cat family *Felidae*. It is best described as the fastest-running ground animal on earth. The cheetah's ability to run an amazing 70 mph is aided by its body characteristics.

Term: cheetah

Section 1
The cheetah is smaller than other big cats. It has a slender, long-legged body that is made for speed. The cheetah has a tan fur coat with round, black spots. It has a small head and ears and distinctive "tear marks" that run from the corners of its eyes down the sides of the nose to its mouth. These stripes keep the sun out of the cheetah's eyes when it is hunting. In addition to a thin, muscular body, the cheetah has a flexible spine, oversized liver, enlarged heart, and increased lung capacity. These all help the cheetah cover 22 to 26 feet with each stride.

Section 1: characteristics

Section 2
The cheetah's speed is important in hunting prey. Unlike other big cats, the cheetah will stalk its prey for three to four miles. Then it finally accelerates and catches its prey. Using its semiretractable claws, it feeds on gazelles, wildebeest calves, impalas, and smaller hoofed animals. The cheetah hunts in the early morning and late afternoon.

Section 2: habits

In addition to sections, the definitive pattern includes nouns like *definition, description, terminology,* and *term.* It includes verbs like *define, describe, designate, mark, name, prescribe, restate,* and *summarize.* Look at **Example 3.** Notice that the word *described* in the first paragraph is important because it is followed by a definition of the term *cheetah.* The word *described* also signals that a description may follow. Now look at **Example 3** again. What important words in the last sentence of the first paragraph signal what is to come in Section 1?

Definitive phrases such as *in other words, that is,* and *that is to say* may be used in the introduction or conclusion. They help to restate the definition or the main idea connected to the definition.

Finally, sections and major items in each section may be introduced with ordering words. These include *first, second, next,* and *finally.* Look at **Example 1.** It has many ordering words. Now look at the other examples. They have no ordering words. When do you think ordering words are necessary?

If a reading selection is made up of a term connected with the main idea, and if it is expanded through a short or long definition, it is an example of the definitive pattern.

The most common section types within the definitive pattern are listed below. You will need this list in order to complete Activity 36 and other activities in this chapter. Many of these will be familiar to you.

Section Types

1. Cause/effect

2. Characteristics/habits

3. Comparison

4. Examples

5. History

6. Problem/solution

7. Process

8. Use

Definitive Pattern

Once you identify the definitive pattern in a reading, you can use these strategies to help you read and understand the material:

1. Read the first paragraph or introduction carefully. Identify the key term. Then look for descriptive adjectives or adverbs that may indicate the author's opinion. Next, read the conclusion carefully to see if the author's viewpoint appears throughout the reading.

2. Scan the rest of the passage. Try to see how the term is developed. Mentally divide the selection into sections.

3. Read the entire selection carefully. As you read, verify the key term. Figure out if the author's viewpoint is the main idea. See if the main idea recurs in each section.

4. As you read each section, look for word clues that show the section type. Then look for ordering words such as *first, second,* and *finally.* These may introduce major items (primary details) in each section. Look for category nouns and whole/part relationships between category nouns that label the major items as a group. Look for individual sentences that expand on the major items somehow.

5. After you have identified the major items in each section, look for major details (secondary details) that support the major items.

6. Reread the selection. Recall the term, the main idea, the sections, and as many major items as you can. Then look to see if the author's viewpoint is captured in the title.

Read the next selection. Use the reading strategies described on page 101. Then write the term being defined. List each section type that follows the introduction. Use the list of section types on page 100. The sections are labeled for you.

Introduction

The cheetah is an endangered member of the cat family *Felidae*. It is best described as the fastest-running ground animal on earth. The cheetah's ability to run an amazing 70 mph is aided by its body characteristics.

Section 1

Before the Ice Age, about 40,000 years ago, the cheetah roamed throughout Asia, Africa, Europe, and North America. Worldwide climate changes later reduced the cheetah population. Inbreeding resulted, which weakened the species. It grew more vulnerable to disease and a decreasing reproduction rate. Cub mortality, declining prey, loss of habitat, poaching, trapping, and shooting further reduced the cheetah population. Eventually cheetahs were placed on the endangered species list.

As a result, only an estimated 9,000 to 12,000 cheetahs remain in the wild. Namibia has the largest population of cheetahs. Smaller populations exist in sub-Saharan African countries and in Iran. These cheetahs thrive in savannas and other open areas where prey is accessible.

Section 2

In these areas, cheetahs live a territorial manner. Females live alone, except to raise a litter of two to four cubs for about 18 months. Male siblings form groups of two or three for life. They hunt together and maintain territories from which they mate.

Term: _____

Section Types

    Section 1: _____

    Section 2: _____

Now try applying this approach to a longer passage. Using your reading strategies, read the selection carefully. On the lines that follow, write the term and the section type. Also list the descriptors in the introduction that show the author's viewpoint.

Many Americans do not function at their best. Their job demands and family issues rob them of a needed seven or eight hours of rest each night. In general, sleep is not a priority for many individuals in our fast-paced society. However, most people *do* realize how much better they feel when they have slept. Understanding the benefits of sleep may help us recognize its necessity.

Sleep is not a dark, empty cavern that we fall into each night. Rather, sleep is a body reaction triggered by the hypothalamus. It acts like a switch, sending chemical messengers through the body. Light traveling from the optic nerve stimulates the hypothalamus area to shut down activity. This action follows the body's biological clock, or circadian rhythm.

Internal factors establish circadian rhythms. They determine "early bird" and "night owl" sleep patterns. Circadian rhythms respond to light. Therefore, individual biological clocks are usually set to the 24-hour cycle of the sun. Circadian rhythms determine how much sleep people need to function. Circadian rhythms dictate when people fall asleep and when they wake up. They also govern functions related to sleep. The hypothalamus sends signals to the pineal gland. This produces melatonin, a hormone that induces sleep. The hypothalamus also regulates body functions related to sleep: body temperature, hormone secretion, urine production, and blood pressure.

However, external factors can cause changes in body rhythms. Circadian rhythms can be disrupted by noise, such as an alarm clock, or by passage into a new time zone. The disorientation and exhaustion that can come from an altered body cycle during air travel is termed jet lag. Circadian rhythms also are altered when bedtime habits or sleep patterns are changed, as in the case of shift workers or night workers. Disrupted sleep patterns usually result in inadequate sleep or insomnia. Related health problems stemming from lack of sleep may occur.

Our internal body clock reminds us to sleep. Sleep revitalizes our body and brain. It enables us to function well.

Term: _____

Section Type: _____

Descriptors: _____

The Main Idea

The main idea in the definitive pattern is the central statement behind the definition. For example, the selection on sleep is written to show that sleep is necessary for good health. In this manner, definitive patterns showcase central ideas. Often, the author's viewpoint is obvious within that central idea.

Because the definition reflects the author's view, the author's bias can often be spotted easily. For example, from the word *necessity,* you can guess that the author views sleep as an important part of each 24-hour cycle.

Sometimes you can find a clear idea of the author's opinion in the first paragraph or introduction. At other times, you will need to look further. Note the author's use of descriptive words. These include adjectives and adverbs, but other word choices can also tell you a lot. Does the author establish a background for the term? Does the author explain the importance of the term?

Understanding the author's view of the term being defined will help you in several ways. If you can tell the author's opinion, you can evaluate it for bias. You can use it to identify the main idea of a paragraph or a longer selection. You can use it later when you need a title for your outline.

Read the selection in **Example 4.** Look for the author's viewpoint both in the first paragraph and in the use of descriptors throughout.

> **Example 4**
>
> Asteroids are metallic, rocky bodies that orbit the sun. These bodies are an enigma to us on Earth. They are too small to be considered planets; yet, they are often known as "minor" planets. Most asteroids are located within a main belt between the orbits of Mars and Jupiter. However, some obscure asteroids have been found within Earth's orbit.
>
> Ceres, the largest asteroid, was discovered in 1801. This object is 933 km in diameter. The next largest asteroids are Pallas, Vesta, and Juno, which measure between 400 and 525 km in diameter. Many asteroids larger than 200 km are known. The others are unknown.
>
> Little is known about the density of asteroids. According to data obtained by the 1997 NEAR-Shoemaker mission, the density of these mysterious bodies is thought to resemble that of water. Asteroids thus do not appear to be solid. Many scientists believe that asteroids are part of an early solar system. They may be leftover materials that never formed into planets.
>
> **Descriptors:** *enigma, obscure, unknown, mysterious*
> **Viewpoint:** Asteroids are mysterious.

Read the next selection. Look for the main idea. On the lines that follow, write the term being defined, key descriptors in the first paragraph, and the main idea.

Comets are mysterious mixtures of frozen gases and water. They seem to be ancient solar-system samples that failed to fuse into planets. Comets are often described as dirty snowballs or icy mud balls. These frozen mixtures orbit the solar system, invisible until they near the sun.

When a comet approaches the sun, its distinct parts can be seen at sunrise or at sunset. These parts are the nucleus, coma, hydrogen cloud, dust tail, and ion tail. Some comets have predictable orbits. They pass by the sun in orbital periods of less than 200 years. These are called *periodic comets*.

One periodic comet, Halley's Comet, was sighted in 240 B.C.E. It was seen again in 1066 C.E., before the famous Battle of Hastings. Centuries later, a scientist named Edmund Halley learned that the comet also appeared in 1531 and 1607. Halley calculated its 76-year orbital cycle. He predicted that this comet would reappear in 1758. Unfortunately, Halley died before the comet arrived, as predicted, on Christmas Eve of 1758. Halley's Comet reappeared in 1835 and 1910. In 1985, a NASA satellite was launched in order to study the comet's arrival in 1986. From the study, the nucleus of the comet was found to be shaped like an ellipse. It measured 16 by 8 by 8 kilometers. Halley's Comet will revisit the earth in 2062.

Another type of comet passes through the inner solar system, then disappears for thousands of years. These comets, like Hale-Bopp, have unknown orbital patterns.

Comet Hale-Bopp first appeared in 1995. Researchers from University of Notre Dame, NASA's Goddard Space Flight Center, and Rowan College determined that the giant comet was formed of frozen water and carbon monoxide. Scientists using Hubble Space Telescope images calculated the comet's diameter at about 40 kilometers. For two years, Hale-Bopp circled the earth. In 2001, it was last sighted by the European Southern Observatory. Then it gradually moved beyond the sun into an unknown path within the vast universe.

Term: _____

Descriptors: _____

Main Idea: _____

Titling the Reading: A Guide to the Main Idea

If a reading selection does not have a title, it is helpful to create one. This can help you identify the main idea. It will also help later when you need to give your outline a title. The title should say what the term being defined is. It should also reflect how the author views the term. Try to keep the title short—no more than five words.

The passage below defines a popular American park. Descriptive words tell how the author is impressed by the park's natural surroundings.

Example 5

Yellowstone is billed as America's oldest national park. Estimated as at least 12,000 years old, this scenic jewel premieres as the home of grizzly bears, wolves, bison, and elk. The park is located in Wyoming, on the site of an active volcano. Yellowstone showcases a variety of natural geothermic phenomena for its visitors.

Yellowstone's most famous attraction is Old Faithful. This spectacular geyser is located in Upper Geyser Basin and fascinates spectators. Nearby, Morning Glory Pool offers an awesome array of colorful, boiling mud pots. Mammoth Hot Springs, another thermal wonder, includes park headquarters along with the oldest park buildings. Yellowstone National Park's natural beauties include Yellowstone Lake, the highest-altitude lake in the continental United States. It also features the Grand Canyon of Yellowstone, with its gorgeous Lower Falls.

The descriptors *scenic, jewel, spectacular, awesome, wonder, beauties,* and *gorgeous* plainly convey the author's opinion. A title like "Yellowstone: A Scenic Showcase" reflects the author's viewpoint.

Titling Strategies

Sometimes it is easy to think of a title for a reading. At other times, you may need to use a system. If you cannot think of a title, try "building" one by following these steps:

1. Identify the term being defined.

2. Find the adjectives or other descriptors that show the author's view of the term.

3. Use the term and one or more descriptors in your title.

4. Limit your title to five words.

Read the selection below. Identify the term being defined. While you read, look for descriptors that show the author's viewpoint or bias. Then title your selection. Write the term, key descriptors, and the title on the lines below the reading.

Eminent domain is the legal right of the government to take privately-owned property for common use. Eminent domain comes from the idea of the "common good." It increases the holdings of state and local governmental organizations. Lands acquired through eminent doman are often used to expand public services to the local community.

However, the exercise of eminent domain often generates controversy. It encroaches on the individual land ownership. When exercised, eminent domain strips property owners of their right to maintain property.

Since eminent domain can be used by the government even if the owner does not wish to leave, it is a volatile legal issue. Even though "just compensation" must be paid to them, property owners often do not respond favorably. Some challenge the government's right to take property. Most, assuming the government will prevail, hold out for higher compensation.

Despite objections, the legal power of eminent domain remains in force. This is because the term *public use,* according to the U.S. Constitution, has been interpreted broadly by state and federal courts. In some cases, the definition of public use has been expanded to include public benefit. Thus, property taken under eminent domain does not have to be available for actual public use. As long as the court sees a public benefit, the property can be acquired.

Term: _____

Descriptors: _____

Title: _____

Naming Major Items

The definitive pattern in longer selections is made up of a term that is defined in various section types:

1. Cause/effect

2. Characteristics/habits

3. Comparison

4. Examples

5. History

6. Problem/solution

7. Process

8. Use

Each section is made up of major items (primary details) and major details (secondary details). Sometimes the different sections and major items are confusing. You need to distinguish between the sections and the set of major items that make up each section.

In the example below, the first paragraph defines the diamond. The next section describes the criteria used to evaluate diamonds. Although each rating standard (major item) has major details, you do not have to remember them all. You just need to understand the basis for the overall evaluation. Remembering the four major items is enough to help you recall how a diamond is rated.

Example 6
Introduction
The diamond, the hardest of all gems, is the purest form of carbon. Over millions of years, its crystals have been formed in the earth's interior. Diamonds are created under enormous pressure and high temperatures. Then they are released to the earth's surface by volcanoes. The diamond's closest relatives are mineral graphite and amorphous carbon.

Term: diamond
Definition: The diamond, the purest form of carbon, is formed over millions of years and is the hardest gem.

Judging a Diamond's Value

The ancients viewed diamonds as sacred in their uncut form. However, modern stone cutters, jewelers, dealers, and manufacturers view them differently. They assess the value of a diamond by its carat weight, clarity, color, and cut.

Carat weight refers to the size of a diamond. It is a unit of weight. A carat is divided into 100 parts, called points. One carat equals 100 points. Half a carat equals 50 points. Diamonds less than 20 points are set as groupings in jewelry.

However, the cut of a diamond may determine the value of its carat size. Even a large diamond, if cut too shallow, will have little brilliance. A diamond cut too deep may appear dark and dull in the center. Thus, the size of a diamond does not guarantee its worth.

> **Major Item (Primary Detail):** carat weight
> **Major Details:** points of carat; cut of diamond

Clarity measures both the external and internal condition of the diamond. Exterior blemishes are the nicks on the diamond facets. They also are unwanted, extra facets; polish lines; and marks on the diamond, or surface graining of the outer stone. Internal flaws, or inclusions, are the presence of clouds, feathers, or mineral crystals within the diamond. Other flaws are internal graining within the diamond or rough surfaces penetrating the inner stone. Blemishes and inclusions are rated by the GIA Clarity Grading Scale. A flawless diamond, free from all inclusions and blemishes, gets the highest evaluation. This, then, is the most expensive diamond.

> **Major Item (Primary Detail):** clarity
> **Major Details:** exterior blemishes; internal flaws

Coloring determines the value of the diamond. Colorless diamonds are rated by the absence of color according to a color scale recognized worldwide. This scale rates ranges in color from the most valued grade D (the absence of color) to grade Z (yellow color). In general, as the amount of yellow in the colorless stone increases, the value of the diamond decreases. On the other hand, color such as blue or red adds value to the diamond.

> **Major Item (Primary Detail):** coloring
> **Major Details:** absence of color rating; yellow decreases value;
> blue or red adds value

Finally, the cut of the diamond helps to define its worth. A diamond properly cut assures its brilliance and its value. The quality of the cut is defined by the diamond's 58 facets. It is judged by the accuracy and precision in the cut proportions. Symmetry of the facet angles is critical, as are the polish and the finish of the cut. Together, these aspects of good workmanship assure a brilliantly cut, expensive diamond.

> **Major Item (Primary Detail):** cut
> **Major Details:** 58 facets; symmetry of angles
> **Section Type:** Characteristics

Unlike short passages, longer definitive readings may be more difficult. You will often have to figure out section types. You will need to sort out the major items and major details in each section. Of course, you should keep track of the major details in each major item. These will be the supporting details in your outline.

In the selection below, note the section type. It will help you understand how the diamond is described. Notice the word *ages* in the first sentence of the second paragraph. What section type does this word suggest? Note, too, how the major items are constructed and named in chronological order.

Example 7
The diamond is defined as carbon in its most concentrated form. It is the oldest item anyone can own. Most diamonds, formed far below the earth's crust, are billions of years old.

The diamond has been prized throughout the ages. Ancient peoples in India three thousand years ago valued the diamond for its ability to refract light. Diamonds mined during that time were used as decorations and as charms for protection in battle.

> **Major Item (Primary Detail):** diamond in ancient times
> **Major Details:** ancient India; decorations; charms for protection in battle

During the early Middle Ages, the diamond was thought to have mystical powers. Diamonds were believed to bring success and luck. They were actually swallowed for healing wounds and curing illnesses. Diamonds were also used as talismans to ward off disease and astrological events. Thus, the diamond became recognized as a symbol of power, fearlessness, and invincibility.

> **Major Item (Primary Detail):** diamond in early Middle Ages
> **Major Details:** mystical powers; symbol of fearlessness and invincibility

Unsurprisingly, diamonds during most of the Middle Ages were reserved for European royalty. An act of Louis IX of France (1214–1270) reserved all diamonds for the king. Within the next 100 years, diamonds were incorporated first in royal jewelry, then in the jewelry of the European aristocrats. Diamonds were given as engagement gifts in the fifteenth century. Maximillian of Austria began the tradition by giving a diamond ring to his fiancée, Princess Mary of Burgundy.

Major Item (Primary Detail): diamond in Middle Ages
Major Details: used in royal and aristocratic jewelry; engagement gifts

By the seventeenth and eighteenth centuries, the diamond was the ultimate gem. It represented power, wealth, and prestige. Before the eighteenth century, India was the only known source of diamond mines. During the eighteenth century, diamond mines were found in Borneo and in Brazil. However, the discovery of the largest diamond fields occurred a century later near the Cothe Orange River in South Africa. These momentous findings unleashed a frenzied diamond rush. It was the birth of the modern diamond industry.

Major Item (Primary Detail): seventeenth and eighteenth centuries, modern age
Major Details: world's diamond mines; diamond rush in South Africa

Word Clues

The definitive pattern may have word clues that relate to the definition. Phrases like *that is, that is to say,* and *in other words* often restate the definition. Verbs like *define, describe, designate, mark, name, restate,* and *summarize* do, too. Nouns such as *definition, description, term,* and *terminology* signal an explanation and the definitive pattern.

After identifying the term, the reader must sort out the section types. Word clues can help in naming each section. There may be whole/part relationships between a section and the paragraph units within the section. This is the case in **Example 7.** Finding this relationship helps you understand the overall section. Category nouns, such as *the comet,* may also name major items, such as Halley's Comet and Comet Hale-Bopp.

Each section type has other word clues that can help you identify the section. Notice that the word clues listed for each section type also can be used as section titles. Many of these words clues are already familiar to you.

Section Type	Word Clue/Section Title
Cause/effect	*cause, effect, reason, result*
Characteristics/habits	*characteristics, facts, habits, items, traits*
Comparison	*advantage, compare, comparison, contrast, differ, difference, disadvantage, opposing*
Example	*entry, example, item, sample, illustration, picture, profile*
History	*after, ancient, ago, before, century, centuries, chronology, chronological, date(s), decade(s), current, millennium, passage, past, period(s), present, span, time, time span(s), universal*
Problem/solution	*clarification, dilemma, predicament, problem(s), resolution(s), solution(s), alternative(s)*
Process/use	*action, end, process, procedure(s), start, step(s), use(s), usage*

Finally, ordering words such as *first, second, next*, and *finally* can help you recognize major items and major details within each section.

Here is another section of the diamond reading. Read the selection carefully. Find the word clues for the section type, and find each major item, or primary detail. Notice that the word clue *example* names a section type. It can also be a section title.

Example 8

The first example is the Cullinan diamond. It is the largest diamond crystal ever discovered. In its rough form, this enormous diamond weighed 3,106 carats, or about 1½ pounds. The Cullinan was discovered on January 26, 1905, in the Premier mine of South Africa. It was named for Sir Thomas Cullinan, chairman of the mining company. The rough diamond was purchased by the Transvaal Government for $750,000. It was presented to King Edward VII of England in 1907 as a birthday present. In 1908, the Cullinan was sent to Amsterdam to be cut. The result—a spectacular, pear-shaped diamond of 530.20 carats—was mounted in the British Royal Scepter. Currently, the Cullinan is the largest cut diamond in the world. It is housed today with the other British Crown Jewels in the Tower of London.

      Major Item (Primary Detail): the Cullinan diamond
      Word Clues: *first, example*

The second example, the Hope diamond, is well known. Its history begins in about 1667 in Golconda, India. There this 112-carat diamond was purchased by Jean Baptiste Tavernier, a French merchant traveler. In 1668, Travernier sold the beautiful violet stone to King Louis XIV of France. In 1673, the stone was recut by the court jeweler to a 67⅛-carat stone. Described in royal records as steely blue, the stone became known as the Blue Diamond of the Crown, or more commonly, the French Blue.

In 1749, Louis XV had the diamond reset by his court jeweler in ceremonial jewelry for the Order of the Fleece. In 1791 the French monarchy fell. The French Blue diamond, along with other court jewels, were taken by the revolutionary government. In 1792, the crown jewels were looted, and the French Blue disappeared.

In 1812, the French Blue resurfaced in England. It was in the hands of a London diamond merchant. Later evidence suggested that the diamond was owned by King George IV of England, then sold privately after the king's death in 1830. In 1839, the French Blue was listed in the inventory of Henry Philip Hope, for whom the diamond is now named. For the next 70 years, the diamond remained in Hope's family. Then it was sold by Hope's grandnephew in 1901. After being sold several times, the Hope diamond was purchased in 1911 by Ms. Evalyn Walsh McLean of Washington, D.C.

Because Ms. McLean did not like the original setting, the Hope diamond was reset as a headpiece. It was set in a three-tiered circlet of large white diamonds as a condition for the 1911 sale. Later, the stone became a pendant on the diamond necklace currently known throughout the world. After the death of Ms. McLean in 1947, the diamond necklace was purchased by Harry Winston, Inc., of New York City. For the next 10 years, the Hope diamond was displayed at many exhibits and charitable events. In 1958, the company donated the Hope diamond to the Smithsonian Institution in Washington.

Today, the Hope diamond weighs 45.54 carats. It is a dark grayish-blue color with a strong red phosphorescence. The Hope diamond setting is surrounded by 16 white diamonds. Its necklace chain contains 45 diamonds. Understandably, it is one of the Smithsonian's most popular exhibits.

Major Item (Primary Detail): the Hope diamond
Word Clues: *second, example*
Section Type: Example

Read the following selection. Determine the section type. Use the chart on page 112 to help you title the section. Then list the major item and major details in each section. You may find it helpful to underline word clues in each paragraph.

Yellow jackets are vicious wasps that look like honeybees. A yellow jacket is about a half-inch long. It has a narrow waist with alternating yellow and black bands on the abdomen. Because yellow jackets eat harmful insect pests, they can be helpful. Home gardeners and commercial growers benefit from them during the spring and summer months. However, during the late summer and fall, the number of yellow jackets grows. At the same time, there is a declining number of insect pests. This creates a hungry yellow-jacket population.

If you are stung, the effect is immediate. Home-remedy treatment should begin right away. First, remove all jewelry near the sting site. Then apply ice to the site in order to reduce pain and swelling. Pastes of meat tenderizer, mud, or baking soda can also be used.

Major Item (Primary Detail): _____

Major Details: _____

Over-the-counter medicines are also available. Benadryl™, for example, is an over-the-counter oral antihistamine. It can reduce pain by counteracting toxins made in the body's reaction to yellow-jacket venom. However, it must be taken immediately. Hydrocortisone cream can also be applied to the sting site, to relieve itching. Most people recover from a sting within two to five days without complications.

Major Item (Primary Detail): _____

Major Details: _____

If you have a violent allergic reaction, you should seek immediate medical attention. Don't delay, especially if you develop hives or if your face begins to swell. If you experience shortness of breath, dizziness, or throat tightness, or if you have difficulty breathing, you need to go to the emergency room quickly.

Major Item (Primary Detail): _____

Major Details: _____

Section Type: _____

Using a Graphic Organizer

You can use a graphic organizer like this one to prepare for making an outline. You will work from the inner circle to the outermost circles of the organizer. Write the term being defined in the innermost circle. Write the main idea in the next circle. If you do not know the main idea, write down one or two descriptors. Next, determine the section type of the first section. Write the section type in the third circle. After you have recorded the first section type, write its first major item in the top, left quadrant of the next circle. Record the other major items in the other circle quadrants, moving in a clockwise direction. Fill in the supporting major details for each major item. Then record the second section type in the fifth circle. In the outermost circle, fill in the major items and supporting major details of the second section, filling in the circle quadrants in a clockwise direction.

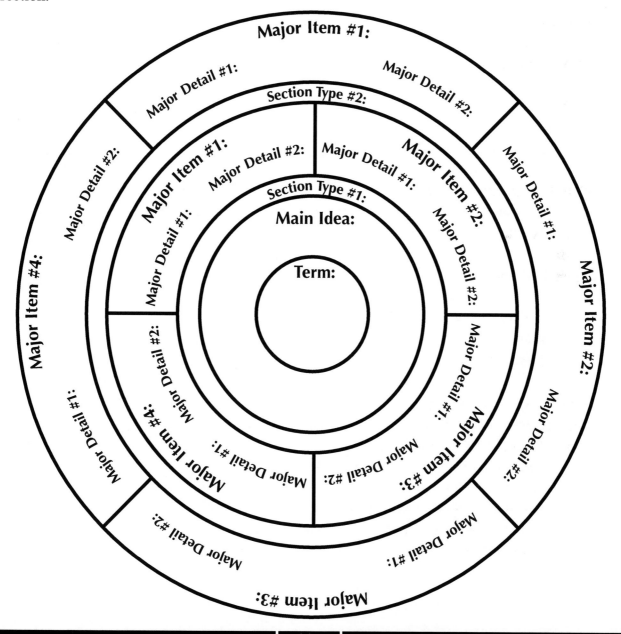

Designing the Definitive Pattern Outline

In the definitive outline, the term being defined is titled. It gets the first Roman-numeral heading. Under the first Roman-numeral heading, major items in the definition are capital-letter entries. Major details are Arabic-numeral entries. The second and third Roman-numeral headings are the section title headings. Ideas for these titles can come from the chart on page 112. Under each of these headings, major items should be listed as capital-letter entries. Next, each major detail is listed as an Arabic-numeral entry under the related capital-letter entry. Minor details are listed as lowercase-letter entries under related Arabic-numeral entries. As always, the outline moves from general to specific as the entries move from left to right.

Examples 7 and **8** give information on the diamond. Here is what an outline based on these examples might look like:

The Prized Diamond
- I. The diamond
    - A. Pure carbon
    - B. Oldest item owned by people
        - 1. Formed in Earth's crust
        - 2. Billions of years old
- II. History of the diamond
    - A. Ancient times
    - B. Early Middle Ages
    - C. Middle Ages
    - D. Modern age
- III. Examples of famous diamonds
    - A. The Cullinan diamond
        - 1. Discovered in South Africa
        - 2. Largest cut diamond in the world
            - a. Originally 3,106 carats
            - b. Now 530.20 carats
        - 3. Mounted in British Royal Scepter
    - B. The Hope diamond history
        - 1. seventeenth century—discovered in India
        - 2. eighteenth century—in French court, known as French Blue
        - 3. nineteenth century—owned by the English Hope family
        - 4. twentieth century—owned by American, Ms. McLean
        - 5. 1958—donated to Smithsonian Institution by Harry Winston, Inc.

Building a Definitive Outline

Building a definitive outline involves combining the steps you have learned in this chapter. You may want to use the graphic organizer to record the information you gather. When the organizer is completed, use it to fill in your outline.

1. Identify the term being defined. Title the term with the first Roman-numeral heading.

2. Find the major items in the definition. List the major items as capital-letter entries under the first Roman-numeral heading. List major details as Arabic-numeral entries under each capital letter.

3. Determine the section types. Title each section, using the Word Clue/Section Title chart as your basis. List each section title as a Roman-numeral heading.

4. List the major items for each section as capital-letter entries. If there are major details, list at least two as Arabic-numeral entries under the related capital letter.

5. If needed, list at least two minor details as lowercase-letter entries under the related Arabic-numeral heading.

6. Finally, title your outline. Try to capture both the term and the author's viewpoint.

Construct a short outline for the next section. Follow the steps listed on page 117. Do not use more than two Roman-numeral headings. Use the chart on page 112, or use word clues within the selection to make your Roman-numeral headings.

Yosemite National Park is located in California's Sierra Nevada Mountains. It was established in 1840 as America's third national park. Yosemite is a showcase of mountain and valley scenery. This national treasure offers visitors a variety of geological wonders: high cliffs, spectacular falls, alpine meadows, and ancient trees.

Like the park's terrain, the wildlife in Yosemite varies widely. Black bears roam the park area, often foraging for food from visitors. Silver-grey coyotes also prowl, feeding on field mice and squirrels. Mule deer graze in the open meadows. Although they may appear tame, their weaponry—sharp horns and hooves—can threaten unwanted visitors. Bighorn sheep, once extinct due to hunting, diseases, and lack of food, also now frequent Yosemite. Occasionally, endangered birds like golden eagles, great grey owls, and peregrine falcons soar through the park area.

Outline Title: _____

    I. _____

       A. _____

       B. _____

       C. _____

   II. _____

       A. _____

       B. _____

       C. _____

          1. _____

          2. _____

       D. _____

       E. _____

          1. _____

          2. _____

          3. _____

Here is a longer reading to practice on. Follow the same steps as you did in Activity 41. This time, though, create your own outline on a separate sheet of paper. Use no more than three Roman-numeral headings. Use the chart on page 112 or word clues within the reading as the basis for your Roman-numeral titles. Remember, proper outline style means that you should not have just one capital-letter and/or Arabic-numeral entry. You must have at least two.

A cup of coffee is a morning must for many adult Americans who wake up daily to guzzle their brew. Most Americans think of coffee as a delightful beverage, not a fruit product. However, coffee comes from a fruit tree—the coffee tree that thrives in temperate climates. At harvest time, coffee fruits are bright red cherries resembling the red grape. Like the grape pit, the green coffee bean can be found within the fruit.

Coffee beans must be processed in order to produce coffee as a beverage. First, local farmers must pluck the coffee fruit by hand from coffee trees that have matured for three to five years. After the fruit is harvested, it may be dried by one of two methods.

The first method is the dry, or "natural," method. It produces beans with a heavier body and a mildly acidic taste. In Ethiopia and Brazil, the dry method is traditionally used. In these countries, the harvested coffee cherries are spread over a concrete block. They dry in the sun, getting raked several times daily. They are covered at night to prevent moisture. After a week to 10 days, the coffee cherries have dried to a dark brown. The fruit is then stripped from the beans with a hulling machine. The dried beans are then stored in silos.

The second method is the wet method. It produces beans with a thinner body and an acidic taste. In Columbia and Costa Rica, the wet method is the preferred method of drying coffee beans. In these countries, the pulp from the harvested coffee cherries is washed away from the coffee bean in large vats. After the beans are cleaned, they are dried in the sun or in drying machines.

After coffee beans have been dried, they are graded. First, they are passed over metal screens that allow certain sizes of coffee beans to fall through. Next, the coffee beans are separated and classified by size. Then the defects, broken beans, black beans, and foreign objects are removed by hand.

The grade of the coffee-bean lot is then determined. Many factors must be considered in grading coffee beans. These include the region, altitude, care during cultivation, type of harvesting, and accuracy in production. For the testing procedure, a small amount of each batch is roasted, brewed, and tasted by a professional. This cup taster, or "cupper," determines the body, acidity, and other batch characteristics.

After the coffee beans have been graded, they are roasted to enhance their final flavor. Because roasting time determines flavor, correctly gauging the roasting is an art. While roasting, beans are heated until they make a popping sound. This releases their aromatic oils and flavors.

Coffee is labeled by a variety of roasts. The lightest roast is sometimes referred to as "cinnamon roast" because its color resembles the spice. It is usually underdeveloped in body and flavor. The American roast, sold in American groceries and restaurants, is another light-medium-roasted coffee. It has more body than the cinnamon roast. The darker roasts are the French and Italian roasts. These are known as strong, flavorful coffees. However, espresso, the darkest roast, is reserved for those who enjoy an extremely strong coffee with an almost burnt taste. This coffee is known for its distinct, sharp flavor. In general, the darker the roast, the more developed the flavor. But, like an overbaked cake, the darker-roasted coffee bean loses its flavor if it is roasted too long. Overroasted coffee beans make bitter coffee.

No matter what one's personal preference, the importance of coffee can be gauged by the flood of coffee makers and machines in American homes, restaurants, and convenience stores. The demand for the traditional cup of coffee as well as coffee drinks like cappuccino, café latte, café au lait, and flavored coffees continues to grow. More variety in flavors and roasts appeals to coffee lovers and only enhances the overall pleasure of coffee drinking.

Recognizing the Pattern

The **integrated pattern** features a combination of section types. You will find the integrated pattern in books, chapters, films, and programs with an overall idea or a key term. In school, the integrated pattern is found in textbook chapters.

In some cases, the integrated pattern is like the general/specific pattern. It presents a general statement that is repeated throughout several sections. For example, an integrated reading on the Vietnam War might include sections on causes of the war, war history, and the effects of the war.

In other cases, the integrated pattern is like the definitive pattern. It revolves around a term that is expanded throughout several sections. For example, an integrated reading on photosynthesis might include sections on the causes, the effects, and examples of photosynthesis.

Integrated selections have three parts. The first part is the introduction. It establishes the background for the general point and/or term. The introduction also presents the main idea. The second part of the integrated selection is the body. It expands on the term and/or the general statement. The body is composed of several sections. Each section serves as a major item. It further enlarges the general statement or the term while developing the main idea. The third part is the conclusion. It usually restates, or reaffirms, the main idea.

Designing the Integrated Pattern Outline

In formal outlines, you do not outline the introduction or the conclusion of a reading. However, the main idea should be stated in one sentence above the first Roman-numeral heading.

Use the same procedure for the integrated outline as you would for the general/specific or the definitive outline. Remember, in the general/specific pattern, the general statement is titled as the first Roman-numeral heading. The major items are titled as a whole as the second Roman-numeral heading. In the definitive pattern, the term is titled as the first Roman-numeral heading. The section types are titled as the following Roman-numeral headings. Use the Pattern Outlining chart below to complete the rest of your outline.

Pattern Outlining

Pattern	Roman-Numeral Heading	Capital-Letter Entry	Arabic-Numeral Entry	Lowercase-Letter Entry
1. Process	Major steps in the process	Substeps	Supporting details	Supporting details
2. Problem/ Solution	Problem titled as the first Roman-numeral heading; solution titled as the second Roman-numeral heading	Major steps in the problem/solution	Substeps	Supporting details
3. Cause/Effect	Cause titled as the first Roman-numeral heading; effect titled as the second Roman-numeral heading	Major cause/ effect	Minor cause/ effect	Minor details
4. Comparison/ Contrast	Purpose titled as the first Roman-numeral heading; items titled as the second Roman-numeral heading	Items	Points	Supporting details

Pattern	Roman-Numeral Heading	Capital-Letter Entry	Arabic-Numeral Entry	Lowercase-Letter Entry
5. General/ Specific	General statement titled as the first Roman-numeral heading; major items titled as the second Roman-numeral heading	Major items	Major details	Minor details
6. Definitive	Term titled as the first Roman-numeral heading; section types titled as subsequent Roman-numeral headings	Major items	Major details	Minor details
7. Integrated	Definitive pattern General/Specific pattern			

The Integrated Outline Organizer

General Statement/Term: _____

Outline Title: _____

Descriptors: _____

_____

Main Idea: _____

_____

Section Types: _____

_____

Major Items

I.

    A. _____   **B.** _____

       1. _____   **1.** _____

       2. _____   **2.** _____

    C. _____   **D.** _____

       1. _____   **1.** _____

       2. _____   **2.** _____

II.

    A. _____   **B.** _____

       1. _____   **1.** _____

       2. _____   **2.** _____

    C. _____   **D.** _____

       1. _____   **1.** _____

       2. _____   **2.** _____

III.

    A. _____   **B.** _____

       1. _____   **1.** _____

       2. _____   **2.** _____

    C. _____   **D.** _____

       1. _____   **1.** _____

       2. _____   **2.** _____

IV.

    A. _____   **B.** _____

       1. _____   **1.** _____

       2. _____   **2.** _____

    C. _____   **D.** _____

       1. _____   **1.** _____

       2. _____   **2.** _____

Integrated Pattern

Once you identify the integrated pattern in your reading, these strategies can help you read and understand the material:

1. Read the introduction carefully. Identify the general statement or the term being defined. Be sure you understand the background. Look for the author's viewpoint and the main idea. Then read the conclusion carefully. See whether you have correctly identified the main idea.

2. Scan the body. See how the term or general statement is developed throughout the selection. Look for the main idea. Block the body of the reading into supporting sections.

3. Read the selection. As you read, verify the term or general statement and the main idea. Read each section carefully.

4. Look for word clues that indicate section type. Look for whole/part listings and category nouns that identify major items. Also look for ordering words like *first, second*, and *finally* that introduce major items or major details.

5. After you have identified the major items in each section, look for major details that support major items.

6. Reread the selection. Confirm the term or general statement, the main idea, and the section types. See if the title reflects the author's viewpoint and the main idea.

Here is a selection to practice on. While you are reading, look for the term or the general statement. Then look for descriptors to help you determine the author's viewpoint and the main idea. Look for word clues that will help you figure out section types and major items. Remember to look on page 112 to review the Word Clue/Section Type chart. Next, fill in the Integrated Outline Organizer. You may not need all of the blanks. Finally, create your own outline on a separate sheet of paper. Add minor details where possible.

While walking in a park, have you ever looked at the tallest, broadest trees and wondered how old they were? What if the trees could talk? Dendrochronology tells the story of trees by their tree rings. Tree rings, or growth layers, relate the annual events of each tree's life. Tree rings are produced by earlywood and latewood. Earlywood is a layer of thin-walled wood cells formed early in the growing season. Latewood is a layer of thicker-walled cells formed later in the growing season. Together, these wood cells form a ring around the entire circumference of the tree. Each tree ring reflects past environmental conditions affecting the overall growth of the tree. These include slope gradient, sun, wind, soil properties, temperature, humidity, and snow accumulation.

Variations in the tree rings can be linked to environmental factors. Uniform variation in stable tree rings reveals favorable climatic conditions, such as good soil and enough moisture. Lack of uniform variation shows the effect of poor climatic conditions, such as poor soil and lack of moisture. Variations in tree-ring width are linked to environmental changes in precipitation, light, temperature, and humidity.

Changes in climate that affect tree-ring formation and tree growth are related to three underlying principles. The first principle states that past climatic conditions affecting past tree-ring formation and tree growth have remained constant. This first principle is often referred to as *uniformitarianism*. It affirms that current natural processes have operated in the past. This concept links past and present climatic conditions.

The next principle is that of limiting factors. It states that plant growth is affected by the most limiting environmental condition. The most limiting climatic condition may impact plants in a wide geographic area.

Finally, there is the principle of aggregate tree growth. It links tree-ring growth to a variety of environmental factors: age-related growth trends, yearly climatic conditions, local occurrences, outside occurrences (such as insect infestation), and random events. When these environmental factors exceed ordinary conditions, they impact tree growth and tree-ring formation. For instance, trees growing on a mountain are more affected by wind than are trees at more ordinary, lower elevations.

In general, dendrochronology recognizes the effects of the environment—temperature, rainfall, wind, climate, and infestation—on tree growth. However, rather than relying upon one tree-ring pattern, dendrochronologists prefer to collect multiple wood samples to study. This is called cross-dating.

Cross-dating is a method used to study the overall effect of the environment on tree growth during a specific time period. For an accurate cross-section of tree samples, cross-dating requires that numerous samples be taken from many trees. If a specific environmental variable is studied, trees displaying the effects of the variable are selected. Through cross-dating, dendrochronology offers valuable ecological insights.

Valuable ecological insight also comes from the study of climate variability. Tree rings record gradual shifts in environmental conditions that current weather records, (observed only over the past hundred years) cannot capture. Because changes in temperature and precipitation show up in tree-ring patterns, tree chronologies offer valuable information about past climate conditions. For example, tree-ring patterns seem to indicate that a warm period, paralleling the warming trend of the twentieth century, existed throughout the earth nearly a thousand years ago. It also appears that a severe drought affected much of North America during the sixteenth century.

As more cross-dating data were collected in the twentieth century, the need for international organization and cooperation grew. The International Tree-Ring Data Bank was formed in 1974 as the central, worldwide repository for original dendrochronological data. The International Tree-Ring Data Bank has become a valuable archive for long-term tree-ring studies. It maintains data and preserves baseline information on the world's oldest trees.

Of these, the giant sequoia tree is the most famous. Located on the western slopes of the Sierra Nevadas in California, giant sequoias are the largest trees in the world. General Sherman, the largest giant sequoia tree, extends 275 feet high and measures 36.5 feet in diameter. Some giant sequoias are considered to be at least 3,200 years old.

The bristlecone pine, however, is really the world's oldest tree. As such, it is the oldest living organism on earth. Stunted and gnarled, this ancient pine is found in the White Mountains of California. Its most aged specimen, the Methuselah Tree, is estimated to be about 5,000 years old. It has been growing since the first annals of recorded history.

The tree rings of bristlecone pines and other ancient trees are diaries of the past. They link us with past eras and their events. Throughout the ages, these trees remain, time-transcending symbols of strength and endurance. They are a story of epic survival.

Here is a selection to practice on. While you are reading, look for the term or the general statement. Then look for descriptors to help you determine the author's viewpoint and the main idea. Look for word clues that will help you figure out section types and major items. Remember to look on page 112 to review the Word Clue/Section Type chart. Next, fill in the Integrated Outline Organizer. You may not need all of the blanks. Finally, create your own outline on a separate sheet of paper. Add minor details where possible.

Until recently, North America was thought to have been populated by Asian peoples. They were believed to have crossed a land bridge near the Bering Strait 11,500 years ago and gradually settled down the North American continent. These Asian peoples, called the First Americans, are presumed to be the ancestors of the modern Indians.

However, recent skeletal findings challenge this theory. These ancient remains support the theory that the first Americans may have sailed to North America in migratory waves before the Asian migration.

Some archaeologists think that the Paleoindians, or pre-Indian peoples, were Europeans. They may have sailed across what is now known as the Atlantic Ocean more than 18,000 years ago. Because the Atlantic was much smaller then, sea levels were as much as 400 feet below current levels. Presently submerged European coastal lands were above water at that time. So these archaeologists say sailing conditions favored crossing the Atlantic Ocean during the last Ice Age.

Although this theory is not widely accepted, some scientists cite a common genetic marker between the Great Lakes–region Indians and Europeans. They see it as evidence of a common European ancestral link.

Advocates of this theory also cite archaeological findings in the eastern United States that may show a European migration before the Siberian crossing. Sites in Kenosha County, Wisconsin, reveal woolly mammoth remains. The animals were butchered by humans more than 13,000 years ago. Another site in Meadowcroft Rock Shelter, Pennsylvania, contains evidence of human occupation dating back as early as 40,000 years ago. Whether peoples of European ancestry first inhabited America is speculative. However, it does appear that American inhabitants may have predated the Asian immigrants by at least 2,000 years.

Another theory suggests that the Paleoindians, descended from Australian Aborigines, were the first Americans. These Australian peoples originated in Africa about 60,000 years ago. Some archaeologists think that they sailed by boat from Australia to Brazil. This theory is supported by the 1975 discovery of Lucia, a mummy in Lapa Vermelha, Brazil.

About 11,500 years old, Lucia's facial features and skull measurements are negroid. They closely match the native peoples of Australia and Melanesia.

Most likely, these ancient Australians were the first wave of South American immigrants. Perhaps they settled in the area now known as Brazil's Serra de Caprivara National Park. There, cave paintings of armadillos—extinct before the end of the last Ice Age—confirm the presence of an ancient people. Evidence of other sites that are at least 13,000 years old (11,000 B.C.E.) exists in Monte Verde, Chile, and at the Cavern of the Painted Rock in Monte Alegre, Brazil.

These sites were inhabited at least 1,000 years before the migration of Asians across the Bering Strait land bridge. However, by 9,000 B.C.E., these Australian peoples were conquered by the Asian ancestors of the modern American Indians. The story of their ultimate extinction is told in the change of skull shape that occurred between 7,000 and 9,000 years ago. Within a 2,000-year period, the skulls of local inhabitants changed from being completely negroid to completely mongoloid. Curiously, this ancient racial change from Australian to Asian features shows in the heads of the surviving descendents of the first Americans. These are the Fuegeans, whose hybrid-skull features show a modern blend of the mongoloid and negroid peoples.

A third theory suggests that the first Americans resembled Polynesian and North Asian peoples. This theory is supported by the discovery of several mummies in North America. The first, the Spirit Cave Man, was found in 1940 in Spirit Cave, near Carson City, Nevada. Over 9,000 years old, it is the mummified body of a man, wrapped in a twisted skin robe with leather moccasins. He is estimated to have been about 45 years old. The Spirit Cave Man was 5 feet, 2 inches tall. He is thought to have died from a skull fracture or from abscessed teeth.

Another skeleton is the Wizard's Beach Man. He was discovered in 1978 in the vicinity of Spirit Cave. Five feet, 6 inches tall, this ancient, robust man is thought to have been vigorous and well-muscled. According to radiocarbon dating, Wizard's Beach Man lived more than 9,200 years ago. He may have died during a severe drought.

Both early Nevada men have similar characteristics: a long, relatively small face and a long cranium. These features sharply contrast with the relatively wider and shorter faces of early Native American people. The skulls of both mummies show a difference in origin. Instead of resembling the ancestors of Native American Indians, whom they predated, both mummies bear the closest skull resemblance to the Ainu. They were the original inhabitants of Japan and Asia.

A later discovery, the Kennewick man, has ignited much interest. Discovered in 1996 in Kennewick, Washington, the male skeleton is estimated to have been of late middle age. He was 40 to 55 years old at death, and he was tall (5 feet, 10 inches). Radiocarbon dating estimated the skeleton's age at 9,500 years old. This means that he lived sometime around 7600–7300 B.C.E. Most important, the ancient skeleton lacks the mongoloid characteristics of the modern Native American. Instead, he exhibits many caucasoid and some unknown characteristics. His dental features, however, signal a probable tie to South Asian peoples.

The 1990 passage of the Native American Graves Protection and Repatriation Act guaranteed the right of Indian tribes to bury the remains of native peoples on federal land if they are tied to native tribes. Thus, controversy over the ownership of the Kennewick Man became immediate. At the crux of this conflict was the question: Was the Kennewick Man the ancestor of Native-American tribes? Native Americans maintain that the Kennewick Man should be reburied as a religious issue. Scientists who wish to study the skeleton have pointed to the skeleton's lack of Native-American characteristics. They question its affiliation with any native tribe. This explosive issue has sparked an intense legal battle over the years. Currently, scientists are allowed to study the bones of the Kennewick Man, but the legal debate over who owns the American past remains.

In recent decades, other ancient skeletons have also been discovered. The most significant find was Buhl Woman in 1989, near Buhl, Idaho. Estimated by radiocarbon dating to be at least 10,675 years old, this mummified skeleton is thought to have died between the ages of 17 and 21. Her skull resembles that of both American-Indian and East-Asian populations. This points to the coexistence of two Paleo-North American populations. However, Buhl Woman, the oldest, nearly complete skeleton ever found in North or South America, was returned to the Shoshone-Bannock Tribe for reburial in 1991. Other recent skeletal finds have been the Prince of Wales man, discovered in 1996, and the Pan-Era Woman, found in 1999.

The story of the first Americans remains elusive. Ancient mummified skeletons hint of the past. Yet, until many more skeletons are found, conclusions will remain speculative. Who were the first Americans? Their bones and skulls hint at peoples whose identities remain frozen in time. Were they one people or waves of several peoples? Ancient skeletal remains cast shadows from the past. The complete story of the first Americans remains an obscure enigma.

Here is a selection to practice on. While you are reading, look for the term or the general statement. Then look for descriptors to help you determine the author's viewpoint and the main idea. Look for word clues that will help you figure out section types and major items. Remember to look on page 112 to review the Word Clue/Section Type chart. Next, fill in the Integrated Outline Organizer. You may not need all of the blanks. Finally, create your own outline on a separate sheet of paper. Add minor details where possible.

Sacagawea was a Lemhi Shoshone Indian. She was born around 1788 near Tendoy, Idaho. As a child, Sacagawea worked very hard and was often beaten. This was customary in the case of female Shoshone children.

In the early 1800s, the Shoshone were in a distressed condition. Having suffered brutal enemy forays, the Shoshone had lost lives and property. Poverty-ridden, the Lemhi Shoshone tribe was wintering near the three forks of the Missouri River, now in Montana, during the fall of 1800. They were violently attacked by a band of Minnetaree Indian raiders from the Hidatsa village armed with guns. The enemy raiders killed most of the Shoshone tribe. They captured Sacagawea to serve as a slave.

Sacagawea was then taken from her Rocky Mountain homeland (now Idaho) to the Hidatsa-Mandan villages near modern Bismarck, North Dakota. She was sold to the Mandan Indians, who continued to enslave her. Later, Sacagawea was won as a prize in a gambling game of chance played by Toussaint Charbonneau. He was a middle-aged white French-Canadian fur trader who lived with the Mandan Indians. Charbonneau claimed Sacagawea, along with another Shoshone woman, as his wife.

In October 1804, the Corps of Discovery, headed by Lewis and Clark, arrived among the Mandan and Hidatsa tribes. They wintered in the area, constructing Fort Mandan. They hired Charbonneau that winter to be a Hidatsa interpreter. At that time, Sacagawea was about 16 years of age, and she was pregnant. On February 11, 1805, after a long, difficult labor, Sacagawea gave birth to her son, Jean Baptiste.

While conversing with Charbonneau, Lewis and Clark learned that Sacagawea knew the Shoshone language. Realizing that they would have to buy horses from a Shoshone tribe in order to travel across land to the Pacific Northwest, they asked that Sacagawea come with Charbonneau as their interpreter. Charbonneau eventually joined the expedition on March 17, 1805. In April 1805, the company, including Sacagawea and her infant son, headed west.

Sacagawea was the only woman to accompany the Corps of Discovery. Her presence, together with that of her baby, "Pomp," convinced Indian tribes that the expedition was friendly. Throughout the journey, Sacagawea was an important resource in recommending plant foods and medicines. She also guided the group through territory that only she was familiar with, and she helped them communicate with the Shoshone tribe.

As the weeks passed, Sacagawea's level-headed, serene behavior became apparent. On May 14, 1805, Clark recorded that a sudden gust of wind nearly capsized the boat and threatened to blow away valuable instruments, papers, books, and medicine. Sacagawea, sitting in the back of the boat, calmly caught nearly all of the articles. On July 14, 1805, Clark noted that Sacagawea recognized the territory from previous travels and recommended a gap in the mountains as being a better route. On July 29, 1805, a flash flood nearly threatened the lives of Sacagawea, her son, Charbonneau, and Captain Clark. On August 14, 1805, Lewis recorded that Charbonneau struck Sacagawea. He received a reprimand from Clark for his abusive behavior. Thus, within a few months, Sacagawea had earned the respect of the expedition party.

On August 12, 1805, Captain Lewis and his company crossed the Continental Divide. The next day, the company found a Shoshone band. On August 17, 1805, Sacagawea and her brother, Chief Cameahwait, had an emotional reunion. A few days later, the expedition purchased horses to complete its journey to the Pacific Coast.

In November 1805, the explorers set up a temporary camp on the north shore of the Columbia River estuary. A Chinook man wearing an otter robe visited the camp. The explorers bought the robe in exchange for Sacagawea's blue-beaded belt. Sacagawea was given a blue coat to replace her belt.

Later in November, the expedition decided on the location of its Pacific Coast winter camp. All members, including Sacagawea, voted in this first recorded election in the Far West. Their camp, Fort Clatsop, was located five miles south of Astoria, Oregon. Named for the Clatsop Indians, the fort was completed on Christmas Day. The explorers celebrated the holiday by exchanging gifts of tobacco and handkerchiefs.

In January 1806, local Indians informed the expedition that a whale had been stranded on a beach several miles south of the fort. Clark, upon assembling a group to find the whale, was confronted by a resolute Sacagawea. She was determined to view the Pacific Ocean. Clark, recognizing Sacagawea's past contributions, allowed her to accompany the others.

On their return journey, Sacagawea guided the group through trails she was familiar with. When the expedition reached the Hidatsa-Mandan villages on August 14, 1806, the trip was over. For his services, Charbonneau was paid $500.33 and 320 acres of land. Sacagawea received nothing.

Charbonneau lived among the Hidatsa and Mandans from 1806 until the fall of 1809. At that time, Charbonneau, Sacagawea, and their son arrived in St. Louis, where they settled for a short time. Later, Charbonneau was hired by the Missouri Fur Company. Toussaint and Sacagawea wished to return to the upper Missouri, so they sold their land to Clark for $100. Leaving Baptiste in the care of Clark in St. Louis to be educated, they arrived at Fort Manuel Lisa Trading Post in South Dakota during the spring of 1811.

Sacagawea died the following year at Fort Manuel on December 20, 1812, of the "putrid fever." She left behind an infant girl, later named Lisette. Two months later, Fort Manual, located on the Missouri River, was attacked by hostile Indians. Because Charbonneau was presumed dead, William Clark became the guardian of both Sacagawea's children.

Although Clark's entry in his 1825–1828 account book confirms that Sacagawea had died, controversy still surrounds her death. Tribal legend still maintains that Sacagawea lived well into old age, dying at age 78 on April 9, 1884, on the Shoshone Wind River Reservation in Wyoming. Although this viewpoint is still popular, it lacks historical proof.

Shrouded in life and death, Sacagawea remains a faceless enigma. It is known that she had a lighter complexion than Charbonneau's other Shoshone wife. However, her physical appearance is unknown, unrecorded by her contemporaries. Yet, her character—her courage, resourcefulness, and resilience—mark Sacagawea as an extraordinary person.

Here is a selection to practice on. While you are reading, look for the term being defined or the general statement. Then look for descriptors to help you determine the author's viewpoint and the main idea. Look for word clues that can help you figure out section types and major items. Remember to look on page 112 to review the Word Clue/Section Type chart. Next, fill in the Integrated Outline Organizer. You may not need all of the blanks. Finally, create your own outline on a separate sheet of paper. Add minor details where possible.

Bioluminescence is visible light that is emitted by living organisms. While it is a unique phenomenon in most of the animal world, bioluminescence characterizes marine life. In the deep ocean where no light exists, most marine animals are luminescent. They emit blue-green or green light, because blue-green light travels well in seawater. A unique exception is the black loosejaw, a deep-sea fish that also produces red light.

This unusual luminescence is produced by a chemical reaction within the marine organism. It involves the oxidation of luciferin by a catalyst, luciferase. In some marine animals, the luciferase acts as an enzyme. It oxidizes luciferen and releases light as a by-product. In other organisms, the luciferin, luciferase, and oxygen are bound together within a single-cell molecule or photoprotein. They require the addition of an ion before light is produced.

Luminescent chemical patterns differ because luceferin types vary among many groups of organisms. Jellyfish, shrimp, fish, dinoflagellates, krill, and fireflies have different luceferin compounds. Yet, similar dietary sources are thought to produce similar luceferin types.

Bioluminescence is also regulated in a variety of ways. In most species, the mechanism is neural control. In these species, the photophores, light-producing organs found on the body and mouth of the ocean marine animal, are connected to the sympathetic nervous system. They are triggered by a neurotransmitter, noradrenaline. In other ocean marine organisms, luminescence may be simply a defense mechanism against an external threat.

In general, the ability to emit and to detect light has provided ocean marine life with distinct advantages. It helps them locate and attract prey, protect against or elude predators, and communicate while mating.

One example of bioluminescent ocean marine life is the lanternfish, found in tropical and subtropical oceans. These fish live deep in the ocean, about 200 to 1,000 meters below the surface of the ocean during the day. They migrate at night, though, to feed on planktonic crustaceans 50 meters below the surface of the ocean.

Lanternfish belong to the family *Myctophidae,* which includes over 230 species. Most adult lanternfish average less than six inches. The lanternfish is most noted for its photophores, kidney-shaped light organs located on its body and mouth. The exact patterning of the photospheres differs according to species.

Within the deep sea, luminescent lanternfish are both diverse and abundant. In comparison, luminescent land animals, including earthworms, millipedes, centipedes, and nemotodes, are rare. The most notable luminescent land animal is the firefly.

Like their marine counterparts, terrestrial fireflies use their luminescence to attract mates and lure prey. Fireflies, also known as lightning bugs, are actually beetles belonging to the family *Lampyridae,* which has about 1,900 species. These flying insects are either black or brown with red, orange, or yellow markings. Fireflies have hard outer skeletons, six jointed legs, two antennae, and a body divided into a head, thorax, and abdomen. The last abdominal segment is its luminescent area. Triggered by glutamate produced by the firefly, this area transmits a bright yellow-green color.

Fireflies are produced by eggs laid in rotting wood or on edges of water areas. These eggs, and later the larvae, are also luminescent. Larvae are thought to glow in order to warn predators that they taste unpleasant. The larvae (and later the adult firefly) are also carnivorous. They eat other fireflies, insect larvae, and snails. After passing through a pupal stage, the adult firefly lives an additional five to 30 days in the same habitat before falling victim to its own predators: birds, frogs, lizards, and spiders.

Thus, both land and ocean animals illustrate how bioluminescence aids in the survival of each species. Bioluminescent signals identify an animal as a member of a particular species. Bioluminescent signals also enable certain animal behaviors that influence interactions between species. Bioluminescence defines extraordinary animals and unusual animal lifestyles.

Here is a selection to practice on. While you are reading, look for the term being defined or the general statement. Then look for descriptors to help you determine the author's viewpoint and the main idea. Look for word clues that will help you figure out section types and major items. Remember to look on page 112 to review the Word Clue/Section Type chart. Next, fill in the Integrated Outline Organizer. You may not need all of the blanks. Finally, create your own outline on a separate sheet of paper. Add minor details where possible.

"What's showing?" we ask when planning our weekend entertainment. This simple question reveals the importance we attach to film-watching as a leisure activity. Modern Americans love movies, television programs, and DVDs. Their passion for motion pictures can be traced in history with the development of cinematography.

Cinematography is the illusion of movement through a rapid projection of picture frames. It can be traced to an early fascination with light and movement. Pinhole images capturing light through a tiny hole interested ancient observers. Pinhole imagery later evolved into the candles and oil lamps of the magic lantern. The magic lantern magnified images much like the modern slide projector and overhead projector. It was used in phantasmagoria shows featuring apparitions and ghosts. Despite the fact that these performances were linked to sorcery and black magic, magic lantern shows spread during the seventeenth century in England, and later during the eighteenth century in America. Thus, by the end of the nineteenth century, the magic lantern was a popular American theatrical phenomenon.

Cinematography, however, lacked motion and sound in the still imagery of the magic lantern. The development of photography was only a piece of the missing link. The first still photograph was taken in 1827. It ushered in later advances in motion-illusion devices: the Phenakistoscope in 1832 and the Zoetrope in 1834.

Gradually, moving photography became a reality. In 1877, Emile Reynaud designed the Praxinoscope. This was a hollow drum that captured inner pictures through a centrally placed mirror as the device spun. A year later, Edward Muybridge introduced motion-picture photography. He captured on film a galloping horse using 12 cameras connected by trip wire. These sequential pictures were widely published in still form and popularized by Muybridge's projector, his Zoopraxinoscope.

During the next years, motion mechanisms improved. In 1882, Reynaud added a projection device to use his Praxinscope for public demonstration. Etienne Jules Marey tried to capture intermittent movement through his photographic gun, capturing birds in flight in 12 shots. However, George Eastman's still camera and celluloid film (1889), later adapted for frame-by-frame motion pictures, marked the most significant advance in motion photography.

With the advent of frame-by-frame celluloid film, modern motion-picture photography was born. In 1892, Thomas Alva Edison, with his assistant, W.K.L. Dickinson, introduced the Kinetograph camera. It featured intermittent movement by using advancing film frames. Single-viewer Kinetoscopes, displaying films through intermittent movement, were also developed by Edison. The first film studio, the Black Maria, was built on the grounds of Edison's laboratories at West Orange, New Jersey, in 1893. There they created film strips for the kinetoscope. In 1895, the Holland brothers set up the first Kinetoscope Parlor in New York City, charging the public to view films like *The Kiss* (1896).

Another noteworthy invention was the cinematographe. This was a combination motion-picture camera/projector developed by Auguste and Louis Lumiere. It launched the motion-picture era. The first motion-picture cinema featured the Lumiere films in Paris on December 28, 1895. Competition ensued when Georges Melies, a French competitor, developed a similar camera and set up the first European film studio in 1897.

Advances in motion pictures continued. Herman Caster and W.K.L. Dickinson (1896) developed a camera and projector using 70mm film format. This produced clearer images. Their company, the American Mutoscope Company, became the most popular film company in America. The renamed American Mutoscope and Biograph Company (Biograph) improved the clarity of its films by introducing the 35mm format in 1903.

During the next 20 years, early movie-production companies—the Edison Company, Biograph, and the American Vitagraph Company—began to produce silent films. Early films included *The Great Train Robbery* (1903) and *The Life of an American Fireman* (1903). *Birth of a Nation* (1915), produced by D.W. Griffith, represented a significant milestone in motion-picture technology.

By the 1920s, the film industry was booming. With film production came the proprietary studio system: exclusive acting contracts, management of filming, control of film distribution, and ownership of popular theaters. Film production was ruled by the five major filming studios: Warner Brothers Pictures (1923); MGM (1924); RKO (1928); Famous Players-Lasky, later Paramount Pictures (1926); and Fox Film Corporation (1935). Three minor studios, Universal Pictures (1912), United Artists (1919), and Columbia Pictures (1924), also competed in making films. Movie stars of this era were Mary Pickford, Douglas Fairbanks, Sr., and Charlie Chaplin.

The 1930s are often referred to as the Golden Age of Hollywood. They marked the advent of sound. Although the sound was often of poor quality, it enhanced dialogue between actors, producing superior films. Two-color and three-color films also were introduced, together with animation. Capitalizing on increased opportunities for sound and color, film genres like gangster films, westerns, and comedies further diversified film production. Films starring Jean Harlow, Greta Garbo, John Wayne, Spencer Tracy, and Gary Cooper belong to this era.

Although the movie industry reflected war themes during the 1940s, many classic films produced during this decade are still regarded as icons of the movie industry. Of these films, perhaps the best known is *Casablanca* (1942). Well-known movie stars Clark Gable, James Stewart, and Rita Hayworth are associated with films produced during this decade.

During the 1950s, film viewing in traditional theaters declined, threatening the existence of the traditional studio system. Even though film production featuring color films, larger screens, and three-dimensional imagery improved during this era, theater viewing could not compete with the outdoor drive-in theaters that flourished. Cheap, exploitive films such as *I Was a Teenage Werewolf* (1957) were produced to appeal to a growing teenage audience. Home televisions also threatened theater-viewing, forcing Hollywood studios to divert their operating base from feature filming to television filming. Television shows such as *I Love Lucy* (1951), *Dragnet* (1954), and *American Bandstand* (1957) made their debut. Stars such as Paul Newman, Marlon Brando, and Marilyn Monroe were featured in 1950s films.

The 1960s brought further decline to movie audiences. This resulted in the re-alignment of the studio system. New ownership, mergers, and conglomerates produced competition, which resulted in lowered movie ticket prices. Although the movie industry declined, several noteworthy films marked this decade: *Cleopatra* (1963), *Doctor Zhivago* (1965), and *The Sound of Music* (1965). Stars Elizabeth Taylor and Richard Burton dominated this era.

The 1970s in film production can be summed up by the advent of the blockbuster movie and two lucrative, landmark films: *Jaws* (1975) and *Star Wars* (1977). Jane Fonda, Robert Redford, and Dustin Hoffman are also associated with this decade.

Blockbuster film hits continued throughout the 1980s and 1990s, promoted by more sophisticated sound systems and by comfortable multiplex theaters. Although films competed with new home entertainment technologies—the videocassette, cable television, and Internet filming—popular film hits such as *E.T. The Extra-Terrestrial* (1982), *Return of the Jedi* (1983), *Jurassic Park* (1993), and *Titanic* (1997) emerged. Movie stars such as Julia Roberts, Kevin Costner, Tom Hanks, and Denzel Washington marked this era.

In the early twenty-first century, the film entertainment industry has gained a new face in the flat-screen televisions and DVD players present in many American households. American entertainment has entered another era, echoing the advances of a century past.

Chapter 1 Note to the Teacher

The process pattern is easy for most students to recognize because of step sequencing. However, some students may experience difficulty understanding the difference between major steps and corresponding substeps. Detailed steps may pose problems for slower readers. Using the graphic organizer to present the pattern may assist students to better understand the overall pattern design. However, some students may require extended use of the graphic organizer and may need additional assistance in recording information within the outlining format.

Activity 1

Process: washing a car **Process Steps:** 1. Prepare bucket of soapy water 2. Sponge car 3. Rinse and wipe car 4. Clean car windows 5. Vacuum car interior

Activity 2

Process: refinishing furniture **Descriptors:** time-consuming, rewarding **Steps:** choose stain; remove finish and clean wood; sand wood; apply stain; apply finish

Activity 3

Process: making apple pie **Descriptors:** delicious, flaky, juicy, favorite treat, highlight **Main Idea:** Apple pie is a delicious treat that is easy to make.

Activity 4

Process: making a baseball **Descriptors:** complex, precise **Title:** The Baseball: Made With Care

Activity 5

Major Step (Primary Detail): drain old oil **Substeps:** park car on level surface; apply brake; run engine; turn off engine; unscrew oil cap; jack up car; place pan under oil-tank bolt; remove bolt; drain old oil **Major Step (Primary Detail):** put on new filter **Substeps:** locate oil filter; put filter-wrench around filter; remove filter; wipe filter mounting; coat rubber gasket with engine oil; screw in new filter **Major Step (Primary Detail):** put in new oil **Substeps:** check owner's manual for oil amount; pour in new oil; check dipstick; check for leaks; dispose of old oil **Process:** changing the oil in a car

Activity 6

Outline Title: Making a Face Mask I. Prepare plaster strips A. Buy plaster bandages at medical supply or art store B. Cut bandages into varying strip lengths II. Apply strips to face A. Use petroleum jelly to coat face B. Apply strips horizontally, then vertically C. Fill in and reinforce areas as needed. III. Let mask dry A. Add more strips as needed B. Remove mask gently after 30–40 minutes C. Leave untouched for 24 hours IV. Decorate mask. A. Seal with clear acrylic sealer B. Paint or decorate with feathers, sequins, or glitter.

Activity 7

Outline Title: Building a Compost Pile I. Plan location A. Not near structure/building B. Close to water/not traffic C. Near wall or tree D. Distant from pine trees/vegetable gardens E. Easy access II. Plan the size A. At least 1 cubic yard/no more than 5 square feet B. Size determines if built with railroad ties/bricks III. Build the compost pile A. Soak ground B. Dig trench and cover C. Alternate layers of compost 1. Nitrogenous materials—manure, fertilizer 2. Carbon materials—leaves, grass, weeds, etc. D. Water between layers E. Turn layers

Chapter 2 Note to the Teacher

The problem/solution pattern is easy to recognize, but it may be difficult for some students to sort out. In more difficult selections in which several problems are cited, some students may not readily identify the problem and its corresponding solution. Other students may experience difficulty in recognizing each major step and corresponding substeps. Using the graphic organizer to present the pattern may help students to better understand the overall pattern design. However, some students may require extended use of the graphic organizer and additional assistance in recording information within the outline format.

Activity 8

Problem: a big, blue ink stain on my best pants **Solution:** removing the stain **Solution Steps:** 1. Forced water through stain to remove ink 2. Applied dry-cleaning fluid 3. Soaked stain in water and ammonia 4. Washed pants in washing machine

Activity 9

Problem: not sure how much maintenance is needed for a new car **Descriptor(s):** *responsible* **Solution Steps:** add antifreeze to radiator; inspect car battery; check cables/battery charge; check wipers, distributor cap, points, spark plugs, and spark-plug cables; check hoses and belts; check air pressure in tires; check tires

Activity 10

Process: peregrine falcon restoration project **Descriptors:** *robbing, random, destruction* **Main Idea:** The peregrine falcon is no longer endangered, because of a successful restoration project.

Activity 11

Problem/Solution: unhealthy hair/revitalizing hair **Descriptors:** *dry, brittle, improper, unattractive* **Title:** Getting a Healthy Hair Look

Activity 12

Major Step (Primary Detail): keep guns away from children **Substeps:** avoid storing guns at home; unload and secure gun in locked location; store ammunition in locked location separate from gun; keep keys away from children **Major Step (Primary Detail):** teach children about the dangers of firearms **Substeps:** teach children not to touch or handle guns; teach them to seek help if they find a gun **Major Step (Primary Detail):** Parents must teach children about gun misuse **Substeps:** Parents must explain that gun violence should not be a way to express emotions; they should warn about media violence as a poor role model; they should stress that healthy conflict resolution does not include gun use; they must teach that gun violence results in death or injury **Problem:** accidental home shootings **Solution:** preventing gun violence at home

Activity 13

Outline Title: Reducing Home Clutter I. Coping with clutter A. Messy living space B. Difficulty finding needed items II. Use it or lose it A. Find a place for everything B. Pick up after yourself C. Give away things you no longer want 1. Give away unworn clothes and shoes 2. Clean out closet regularly

Activity 14

Outline Title: Keeping Your Brain Sharp I. Experiencing memory lapses II. Good practices A. Sleep B. Eating well 1. Cutting down on refined carbohydrates 2. Eating high-protein food C. Taking multivitamins and mineral supplements D. Physical exercise 1. "Clears brain" 2. Creates feeling of well being E. Mental exercise 1. Reading 2. Playing piano 3. Thinking games G. Learning strategies 1. Verbal 2. Auditory 3. Kinesthetic

Chapter 3 Note to the Teacher

The cause/effect pattern is initially easy to recognize, but it may be difficult for some students to analyze and sort out. In difficult selections, some students reading at a lower level may confuse the cause with its effect. Other students may experience difficulty in identifying the major cause or major effect and corresponding minor causes and/or minor effects. Some students may not be able to assign minor causes and/or minor effects to their corresponding major cause and/or major effect. Using the graphic organizer to present the pattern may help your students better understand the overall pattern design. However, some students may require extended use of the graphic organizer and additional assistance in recording information within the outline format.

Activity 15

Topic: good skin care **Cause:** eating healthy foods **Effects:** skin is soft and attractive; defends body from disease; protects internal organs; regulates body temperature; prevents fluid loss; helps body remove excess water and salts

Activity 16

Topic: Identity theft **Descriptors:** malicious, vicious **Causes:** carelessness, negligence, lack of perception **Effects:** life of misery: seized money, credit, and good name

Activity 17

Topic: athletic competition—allows for character development **Descriptors:** *good, properly, right, personal, supports, encouraged* **Main Idea:** Good sportsmanship results from good behavior of team members during competitive sports.

Activity 18

Topic: tornadoes **Descriptors:** *deadly, destructive* **Title:** Deadly Storms

Activity 19

Topic: tsunamis **Major Cause:** vertical movement of ocean floor during an earthquake **Major Effect:** altered water waves **Minor Effect (Primary Detail):** low seismic activity in American Atlantic Coast **Minor Detail:** no tsunamis in eastern United States, only recorded tsunami on North American Atlantic Coast in 1929 in Newfoundland **Minor Effect (Primary Detail):** West Coast affected by tsunamis from South American and Alaskan earthquakes **Minor Detail:** 1964 Alaskan quake produced 20-foot waves in California, resulting in $7.5 million damage and 11 deaths. **Minor Effect (Primary Detail):** Alaska is source of earthquakes and tsunamis because of plate activity **Minor Detail:** Alaska rests on colliding Pacific and North American tectonic plates, four major tsunamis there **Minor Effect (Primary Detail):** Hawaiian Islands have many tsunamis due to location in Pacific Ocean **Minor Detail:** 90 percent of tsunamis occur in Pacific; in 1869 and 1975, Hawaiian Islands had waves up to 59 feet

Activity 20

Outline Title: Delayed Retirement: Impacts on American Seniors I. Causes A. Decline in senior mortality rate 1. Improved medical treatment 2. Lack of widespread disease 3. Personal eating/exercise habits B. Reduction in wages versus benefits paid out II. Effects A. Increase of retirement age to 67 B. Concerns about physical ability to work longer C. Availability of post-retirement jobs with health benefits D. Careful financial planning

Activity 21

The West Nile Virus Outbreak I. Cause: Virus as an animal/public health threat A. History 1. 1937—virus isolated in feverish women in Uganda 2. 1950s—virus recognized as cause of encephalitis 3. 1999—encephalitis linked to West Nile virus reported to CDC B. Transmission to animals by mosquito 1. Birds—high virus levels in bloodstream 2. Dead crows show presence of virus. C. Transmission to humans by mosquito II. Effect: West Nile encephalitis A. Symptoms 1. Mild symptoms—fever, headache, aches, rash, swollen glands 2. Severe symptoms—high fever, stiff neck, coma, convulsions, paralysis, death B. Treatment—prompt medical attention C. Prevention 1. Reduced outdoor activity 2. Repellent and protective clothing

Chapter 4 Note to the Teacher

The comparison/contrast pattern may be more difficult for students reading at a low level. Extrapolation is necessary in understanding the purpose for the comparison, the items of comparison, and the points corresponding to each item. Using the graphic organizer to present the comparison/contrast pattern may help your students understand the overall pattern design. However, proceed through this chapter slowly, making sure that your students understand the purpose for the comparison. They should be able to identify items and points within the comparison. Some students may require extended use of the graphic organizer and additional assistance in recording information within the outline format.

Activity 22

Overall Comparison: 1950s dress/today's dress **Items Compared:** dress standards, popular clothes, never/rarely worn clothes, alternatives **Points:** rigid standards/no standards; skirts and dresses/jeans and shorts; circular skirts/low-cut jeans; shorts/skirts and dresses; Bermuda shorts and pedal pushers/dress pants

Activity 23

Overall Comparison: life in the 1950s/life today **Items Compared:** men's clothing, boys' clothing **Points:** uniform society/diverse society; breadwinner role/shared role; subdued and formal business suit/varied colors, styles, and fabrics; formal dress/casual dress; hats/caps; little men/boy look; preppy look/casual look; dress pants/jeans

Activity 24

Comparison: ice cream flavors/personality types **Descriptors:** *unique, clever* **Main Idea:** According to a survey, ice cream flavors can be linked to different personality types.

Activity 25

Comparison: Vinson Massif/Mount Kilimanjaro **Descriptors:** *challenges, adventurous* **Title:** Two Challenging Summits

Activity 26

Items: miniature poodle/Siberian husky **Points (Primary Details):** origin, behavior, appearance **Supporting Details:** Germany, Russia, France/northeastern Siberia; nonsporting/working dog groups; trainable/not easily trained; watchdog/quick, light on feet; curly, dense hair/soft, dense undercoat, outer coat; dark eyes/blue or brown eyes

Activity 27

Roommate War I. Anna A. Sloppy habits B. Noisy 1. Listens to music 2. Talks on phone C. Goes to bed after midnight, rises late II. Roommate A. Neat habits B. Quiet C. Goes to bed at 10, rises early 1. Turns on light 2. Watches television

Activity 28

Candy: An Enticing Treat I. Non-chocolate candy A. History 1. Early humans—honey 2. Egyptians, Arabs, Chinese—confections of fruit, nuts, and honey 3. Middle Ages—sugar 4. England/Early America—boiled sugar candies B. Current Types 1. Hard candy 2. Sugar-coated candy 3. Chewy candy *etc.* II. Chocolate candy A. History 1. 1492—Columbus learns about cocoa bean 2. Cocoa bean transformed into confection 3. Milk chocolate was produced 4. 1868—boxes of chocolates 5. 1900—milk-chocolate bar B. Current types 1. Chocolate candy of all varieties 2. Chocolate cookie bars 3. Chocolate ice-cream bars

Chapter 5 Note to the Teacher

The general/specific pattern is the most common reading pattern. However, some students reading at a lower level may experience difficulty identifying the main idea. Others may have trouble differentiating between the supporting major items (primary details) and their corresponding supporting (secondary) details. Using the graphic organizer to present the general/specific pattern may help students better understand the overall pattern design. However, some students may require extended use of the graphic organizer and additional assistance in recording information within the outline format.

Activity 29

General Statement: North Dakota has many natural resources. **Category Word:** *resources* **Major Items:** petroleum, lignite, sand/gravel, gas

Activity 30

General Statement: The history of ice cream is a long one. **Descriptors:** *smooth, sweet, delicious* **Major Items:** ancient times to eighteenth century (spread around world); nineteenth century (manufacturing); twentieth century (variety)

Activity 31

General Statement: Ancient Scandinavian holiday traditions emphasized warmth and light. **Descriptors:** *ancient, dark, cold, old* **Main Idea:** Ancient Scandinavian holiday traditions emphasized warmth and light (same as general statement).

Activity 32

General Statement: Christmas traditions can be traced over a thousand years. **Descriptors:** *modern, ancient* **Title:** Ancient Customs Shape Modern Christmas Celebrations

Activity 33

Major Item (Primary Detail): team players **Major Details:** offensive field players; defensive goalie **Major Item (Primary Detail):** rules of play **Major Details:** handle ball with one hand; observe specific regions for certain rules of play **General Statement:** Water polo is a popular water sport featuring offensive and defensive players and rules.

Activity 34

Outline Title: Chocolate: Food for the Gods
I. Chocolate—not a health hazard II. Misrepresentations
A. Associated with weight gain/eating disorders 1. Not a cause of eating binges 2. Nutritious—rich in potassium/magnesium B. Associated with acne
C. Associated with high caffeine level D. Associated with allergies

Activity 35

(Note: not all Arabic-numeral entries are included)
Saving Money to Earn More Money
I. Saving to invest II. Types of investments A. Owning home B. Savings/money market accounts C. CDs
D. 401(k) plans 1. Employer—matching funds contribution
2. Tax-deferred 3. Penalty for early withdrawal
E. Stocks/bonds

Chapter 6 Note to the Teacher

The definitive pattern is the most difficult pattern. It incorporates other patterns as pattern parts or sections. Students with low reading levels may experience difficulty staying on task and recognizing how sections relate to the overall definitive design. Because recognition of sections is crucial to understanding the overall design, a short review of the pattern types may be necessary before introducing the definitive design. Then proceed through this chapter slowly, making sure that your students understand that definitive design revolves around one term and that each section is composed of major items related to its own specific pattern. Using the graphic organizer to present the definitive pattern may help students better understand the overall pattern design. However, some students may require extended use of the graphic organizer and help in recording information within the outline format.

Activity 36

Term: cheetah **Section Types:** Section 1: Cause/effect, Section 2: Characteristics/habits

Activity 37

Term: sleep **Section Type:** Cause/effect **Descriptors:** *benefits, necessity, revitalizes*

Activity 38

Term: comets **Descriptors:** *mysterious, ancient, frozen, invisible* **Main Idea:** Comets, frozen bodies of gas and water, orbit in sometimes predictable, sometimes unknown patterns.

Activity 39

Term: eminent domain **Descriptors:** *legal right, common good, controversy, strips, volatile, challenge, prevail, hold out, objections* **Title:** Eminent Domain: A Controversial Power

Activity 40

Major Item (Primary Detail): home-remedy treatment for stings **Major Details:** remove jewelry; apply ice; use meat tenderizer, mud, or baking soda pastes **Major Item (Primary Detail):** over-the-counter medicines **Major Details:** Benadryl™; hydrocortisone cream **Major Item (Primary Detail):** violent reaction **Major Details:** hives; swelling face; shortness of breath; dizziness; difficulty breathing **Section Type:** Cause/effect (reaction to sting)

Activity 41

Outline Title: Yosemite: A National Showcase I. Yosemite National Park A. Located in California's Sierra Nevadas
B. Established in 1840 as America's third national park
C. Includes many geological wonders II. Wildlife
A. Black bears B. Coyotes C. Mule deer 1. Appear tame
2. Sharp horns and hooves D. Bighorn sheep
E. Endangered birds 1. Golden eagles 2. Great grey owls
3. Peregrine falcons

Activity 42

Your Delightful Cup of Coffee I. Coffee A. Originates from coffee tree B. Coffee bean in coffee fruit ("cherry")

II. Processing the coffee bean A. Pick coffee fruit from tree B. Dry coffee beans 1. Dry or natural method (Ethiopia, Brazil) a. Dry in sun b. Rake fruit and cover to prevent moisture c. Strip fruit from beans d. Store fruit in silos 2. Wet method (Columbia, Costa Rica) a. Wash fruit pulp from coffee beans in vats b. Dry coffee beans in sun or drying machines C. Grade coffee beans 1. Grading factors a. Region b. Altitude c. Care d. Type of harvesting e. Accuracy of production 2. Testing procedure D. Roast coffee bean 1. Roasting time/flavor 2. Types of roasts a. Light roast—cinnamon b. Light-medium roast—American c. Darker roast—French/Italian d. Darkest roast—espresso III. Importance of coffee A. Widely popular B. Variety of coffee drinks, flavors, and roasts today

Chapter 7 Note to the Teacher

The student must be able to recognize and identify section types within the definitive pattern before attempting this chapter. Pattern integration demands a thorough understanding of the general/specific and definitive pattern designs and may require a review of both pattern types. Students may experience difficulty recognizing an overall general point or identifying a term pertaining to the entire selection. Also, students may need additional practice in recognizing patterns as section types.

If necessary, review pattern designs with your students and proceed slowly. Make sure your students are able to identify major items and major detail within each section.
Using the graphic organizer to present the definitive pattern may assist your students in better understanding the overall pattern design. However, some students may require extended use of the graphic organizer and additional assistance in recording information within the outline format.

Activity 43

(Only Roman-numeral headings and capital-letter entries are listed.)
It's All in the Rings I. Dendrochronology A. Tree rings B. Reflection of environmental conditions II. Tools of dendrochronology A. Tree-ring formation/tree growth B. Principles underlying dendrochronology C. Cross-dating techniques D. Ecological insights III. Examples A. Giant sequoia B. Bristlecone pine

Activity 44

(Only Roman-numeral headings and capital-letter entries are listed.)
Who Was First? I. Traditional theory names Asians as first Americans. A. Asian peoples crossed a land bridge near the Bering Strait. B. Asian peoples settled down the North American continent. C. Asian peoples are thought to be ancestors of the modern Indians. II. Other theories suggest that first Americans came in migratory waves.
A. Europeans may have sailed across the Atlantic Ocean.
B. Australian peoples may have settled South America.
C. North Asian peoples are thought to have predated ancestors of the North American Indian. III. Despite archaeological evidence, findings remain inconclusive.

Activity 45

(Only Roman-numeral headings and capital-letter entries are listed.)
Sacagawea: Woman of Courage I. Life A. Early years B. Exploration Years C. Post-exploration years
II. Character A. Courage B. Resourcefulness C. Resilience

Activity 46

(Only Roman-numeral headings and capital-letter entries are listed.)
Lights in the Deep I. Bioluminescence is a unique phenomenon found in the animal world.
A. Bioluminescence characterizes ocean animals.
B. Animals have different luminescent chemical patterns.
C. Animals have different luminescent-control mechanisms.
D. Bioluminescence provides many advantages to ocean marine life. II. Two animals are bioluminescent.
A. Oceanic example: the lanternfish B. Terrestrial example: the firefly

Activity 47

(Only Roman-numeral headings and capital-letter entries are listed.)
History of the Cinema and Its Films I. History of cinematography and filming A. Pinhole images B. Magic lantern C. Motion-illusion mechanisms D. Moving photography E. Motion pictures II. History of the film industry A. Before 1920 B. 1920s C. 1930s D. 1940s E. 1950s F. 1960s G. 1970s H. 1980s–1990s I. Twenty-first century

Formal Outline Format

The Topic Outline

To build a **topic outline,** you arrange corresponding headings by order of importance. Together, these headings form a whole-to-parts relationship throughout the outline. The most common example is the **item-list outline.** In this outline, *at least two main items* are listed as *Roman-numeral headings.* Specific details relating to any main items are listed under their Roman-numeral headings as *capital-letter entries.* Parallel capital-letter entries should be used if similar details are cited under other Roman-numeral headings. Likewise, details relating to any capital-letter entries are listed under these headings as *Arabic-numeral entries.* Further details relating to any Arabic-numeral entries are listed as *lowercase-letter entries.*

In the example below, note the parallel construction of corresponding headings. Also, the first word within each heading or entry is capitalized. There are at least two headings for each heading type. Each level of heading is indented further to the right as it decreases in importance.

Item-List or Topic Outline Example
Bear Facts
I. Brown bear (*Ursus arctos*)
   A. Physical characteristics
      1. Large size
         a. 500-to-900-pound adult males
         b. 375-pound adult females
      2. Appearance
         a. Usually brown fur
         b. Long, straight claws
   B. Distribution
      1. Stable population in Alaska and western Canada
      2. Limited population in Europe and Asia
II. Black bear (*Ursus americanus*)
   A. Physical characteristics
      1. Medium size
         a. 130-to-660-pound adult males
         b. 90-to-175-pound adult females
      2. Appearance
         a. Usually black fur
         b. High-curved, strong claws
   B. Distribution
      1. Stable population in forested areas of North America
      2. Isolated population in tundra of northern Labrador

The Sentence Outline

The **sentence outline** is another type of formal outline. In this case, sentence headings are used instead of topic headings. The outline format is otherwise the same as that of the item-list/topic outline.

Sentence Outline Example
Bear Facts

I. The brown bear is a member of the species *Ursus arctos*.
  A. The brown bear has unique physical characteristics.
    1. The brown bear is a large-sized animal.
      a. Adult males range from 500 to 900 pounds.
      b. Adult females average 375 pounds.
    2. The brown bear has striking characteristics.
      a. Most brown bears have dark-brown fur, but may have blond or black fur.
      b. Brown bears have long, straight claws.
  B. The brown bear may be found in many areas.
    1. A stable population is located in Alaska and in western Canada.
    2. A limited population is found in Europe and in Asia.
II. The black bear is a member of the species *Ursus americanus*.
  A. The black bear has unique physical characteristics.
    1. The black bear is a medium-sized animal.
      a. Adult males range from 130 to 660 pounds.
      b. Adult females range from 90 to 175 pounds.
    2. The black bear has striking characteristics.
      a. Most black bears have black fur, but may have chocolate or cinnamon fur.
      b. Black bears have high-curved, strong claws.
  B. The black bear may be found in many areas.
    1. A stable population is located in the forested areas of North America.
    2. An isolated population is found in the tundra of northern Labrador.

Adventures in Cybersound. Britannica Online. 7 November 2002. www.acmi.net.au/AIC/CINEMA_BRITANNICA.html.

Alpine Ascents International. *Frequently Asked Questions.* Alpine Ascents International. 24 July 2002. www.alpineascents.com/fas.asp.

Anderson, Irving W. "The Sacagawea Mystique: Her Age, Name, Role and Final Destiny." *Columbia.* Fall 1999. 3 November 2002. www.wshs.org./Columbia/0399-al.htm.

Asher, Lara. "Oldest North American Mummy." *Archaeology.* September/October 1996. 17 September 2002. www.archaeology.Org/9606/Newsbriefs/html.

Asteroid Introduction. Solarviews. 29 August 2002. www.solarviews.com/eng/asteroid.htm.

Asteroids. Students for the Exploration and Development of Space. 29 August 2002. www.sed.org/nineplanets/nineplanets/asteroids.html.

Bank of America. *IRA.* Bank of America. 1999.

Bauer, Bruce. *The International Tree Ring Data Bank.* Henri D. Gissino-Meyer's Science of Dendrochronology Web Page. 13 October 2002. http://web.Utk.edu/~grissino/itrdb.htm.

Bioluminescence. Naval Meteorology and Oceanography Command. 21 September 2002. http://pao.cnmoc.navy.mil/educate/neptune/quest/marine/biolumin.htm.

Bioluminescence Questions and Answers. Scripps Institution of Oceanography. 30 September 2002. http://siobiolum.uced.edu/Biolum_q&a.html.

The Bioluminescence Web Page. University of California Santa Barbara. 30 September 2002. http://lifesci.ucs.edu/~biolum.

Brain Food. iVillage. 9 July 2002. www.ivillage.com/diet/features.

Branham, Marc. *The Firefly Files.* Ohio State University. 30 September 2002. http://iris.bioscioohio-state.edu/projects/ffiles/frfact.html.

"Buhl Woman." *Archaeology.* November/December 1998. 20 September 1996. 17 September 2002. www.archaeology.org/9609/Newsbriefs/Nevada.html.

Building a Compost Pile. North Haven Gardens. 18 November 2002. www.nhg.com/compost.htm.

Burns, Paul T. *The Complete History of the Discovery of Cinematography.* Planetel Communications. 7 November 2002. www.precinemahistory.net.

Butterfield, Bonnie. *Captive, Indian Interpreter, Great American Legend: Her Life and Death.* Geocities. 3 November 2002. www.geocities.cm.collegePark/Hall9626/NativeAmericans.html.

Bye, Kadie. "Investing Early Garners Huge Rewards For Students." Young Money. 14 August 2002. www.youngmoney.com/stockholder.

Candy History! Online Candy Super Store. 4 August 2002. www.ieatcandy.com.

Castleman, Mike. "How Experts Cope With Stress." *Readers Digest.* November 1994. 140+.

Character Counts! Coalition. *Pursuing Victory with Honor.* Josephson Institute of Ethics. 24 July 2002. www.aforbw.org.

Chatters, James C. "Northern Clans, Northern Times." *Smithsonian.* 1997. 16 September 2002. www.mnh.si.edu/arctic/html/kennewick_man.html.

Cheetah. Kid's Planet. 25 August 2002. www.kidsplanet.org/factsheets/cheetah.html.

Cheetah Facts. Cheetah Outreach. 25 August 2002. www.cheetah.co.za.

The Cheetah Spot. The Cheetah Spot. 25 August 2002. www.cheetahspot.com/appearance.html.

Chicago Coffee Roastery: Coffee Processing. Chicago Coffee Company. 10 September 2002. www.chicagocoffee.com.

Christmas in Scandinavia. Worldwide Online. 8 August 2002. www.wsmail.order/com/Christmas/Scandinavia.htm.

Coder, Kim D. *Tree Growth Rings: Formation and Form.* University of Georgia. 13 October 2002. http://forestry.uga.edu/warnell/service/library/for99-020/index.

Coffee Facts: From the Plantation to Your Cup. Cup of Coffee. 10 September 2002. www.cupofcoffee.com/pages/plantation.htm.

Coffee Tree to Coffee Beans. PageWise. 10 September 2002. www.allsands.com/Food/coffeetreebean_stg_gn.htm.

Color and Design in Your Garden. Lowe's. 21 November 2002. www.lowes.com.

Comet Hale-Bopp. European Southern Observatory. 1 September 2002. www.eso.org/outreach/info-events/hale-bopp.

Comet Hale-Bopp. California Institute of Technology. 29 August 2002. www.jpl.nasa.gov/comet.

Comets. Students for Exploration and Development of Space. 29 August 2002. http://seds.ipl/Arizona.edu/nineplanets/nineplanets/comets.html.

Cough. iVillage. 9 July 2002. www.ivillage.com/diet/features.

Day, Cynthia. *Astronomer Helps Pinpoint Birth/History of Hale Bopp.* University of Notre Dame. 1 September 2002. www.jpl.nasa.gov/Comet/news105.html.

Dendrochronology. Sonicnet. 13 October 2002. www.sonic.net/bristlecone/dendro.html.

Design Your Own Dream Garden. iVillage. 21 November 2002. www.ivillage.com.

Detroit Medical Center. *Cardiovascular Conditioning: Why Is It Important?* Wayne State University. 28 July 2002. www.dmc.org/health_info/topics/exer.3009.html.

Diner's Digest. CuisineNet. 4 December 2002. www.cuisine.net.com/digest/custom/etiquette/tips_pitfalls.shtml.

Dirks, Tim. *The Greatest Films.* Filmsite.org. 7 November 2002. www.filmsite.org.

Driving Tips: Driving on Ice. Roadrangers.com. 2 December 2002. www.Roadrangers.com/tips/driving-on-ice.htm.

Dutton, Gary. *The Four C's for Choosing Diamonds.* Dutton's Diamonds. 4 September 2002. www.diamondexpert.com/articles.

Dvernik, Christine. *Make a Paper Mache Piggy Bank.* Familyeducation.com. 19 November 2002. www.familyeducation.com/article/0112.201467500.html.

Earthquake Hazards Program. *Frequently Asked Questions.* U.S. Geological Survey. 27 July 2002. www.earthquake.usgs.gov/fac.effects.html.

Edelmann, Ric. *Becoming Wealthy One "Bite" at a Time.* Your Financial Planner. 14 August 2002. www.ricedelman.com/planning/basics/wealthybite.asp.

Edelmann, Ric. *The Four Steps To Properly Setting Goals.* Edelman Financial Services. 14 August 2002. www.ricedelman.com/planning/onyourown/4steps.asp.

Edison Motion Pictures. Library of Congress. 7 November 2002. http://lcweb2.log..gov/ammem/edhtml/edmvhm.html.

Edwards, Roger. *The Online Tornado FAQ.* Storm Prediction Center. 24 July 2002. www.spc.noaa.gov/faq/tornado.

Eide, Sterling and Sterling Miller. *Brown Bear.* Alaska Department of Fish and Game. 11 June 2003. www.state.ak.us/adfg/notebook/biggame/brn.bear.htm.

Encyclopedia Smithsonian: Hope Diamond. Smithsonian Institution. 3 September 2002. www.si.edu/resources/faq/nmnh/hope.htm.

Everything About Kwanzaa. The International Kwanzaa Exchange. 8 August 2002. www.tike.com/celeb-kw.htm.

Fabric Stain Guide. Fabriclink. 27 November 2002. www.fabriclink.com/Fabricstains/Inkpermanent.html.

Farewell, Monkey. ABC News. 24 July 2002. http://abcnews.go.com/sections/science/DailyNews/monkey000912.html.

Fauber, John. "Kenosha Dig Points to Europe As Origin of First Americans." *Milwaukee Journal Sentinel Online.* March 3, 2002. 18 September 2002. www.Jsonline.com/news/state/mar0224849.asp.

Federal Trade Commission. *ID Theft: When Bad Things Happen to Your Good Name.* Federal Trade Commission for the Consumer. 3 January 2004. www.ftc.gov/hcp/conline/pubs/credit/idtheft.htm.

Feldman, Elaine B. "Death by Chocolate: Facts and Myths." *Nutrition Today.* May/June 1998. 21 August 2002. www.findarticles.com.

Firefly or Lightning Bug. Enchanted Learning. 1 October 2002. www.Enchantedlearning.com/subjects/insects/beetles/Fireflyprintout.html.

"First Americans Were Australian." BBC Online Network. August 28, 1999. 18 September 2002. http://news.bbc.uk/1/hi/sci/tech.

Geophysical Institute. *The Great William Sound Earthquake of March 28, 1964.* University of Alaska Fairbanks. 28 July 2002. www.aeie.alaska.edu/seis/64quake/quake_description.html.

Goodbye, Miss Waldron. Wildlife Conservation Society. 24 July 2002. http://Home.conceptsfa.nl/~pmasa/miswaldrons-redcolobus.htm.

Grahame, John D. and Thomas D. Sisk, editors. *Canyons, Cultures and Environmental Change: An Introduction to the Land Use of the Colorado Plateau.* 1 November 2002. www.cpluhna.nau.edu.

Grieger, Lynn. *Better Skin Diet.* iVillage. 20 July 2002. www.iVillageHealth.com/features.

Grossman, Hillard. "The Making of a Major League Baseball." *Florida Today.* August 16, 2002. 13 November 2002. www.floridatoday.com.

Growing/Processing. Sun Maid. 13 November 2002. www.sun-maid.com/Growing.html.

Guest Etiquette. Western Silver. 4 December 2002. www.westernsilver.com/Guestetiquette.html.

Guns and Children. American Academy of Pediatrics. 4 December 2002. www.Aap.org/advocacy/childhealthmonth/Guns.htm.

Haddock, Vicki. *Tips for a Better Memory.* iVillage. 9 July 2002. http://aolsve.Health.Webmd.aol.com/content/article.

Haley's Comet. Solarviews. 29 August 2002. www.solarviews.com/eng/halley.htm.

Hall, Don Alan. "The Men from Spirit Cave and Wizard's Beach: Remarkable Discoveries." *Mammoth Trumpet*. December 1997. 17 September 2002. www.cabrillo.cc.us/~crsmith/spiritman2html.

Hill, Art. *Cholesterol & HDL & LDL*. MindbodyHealth. 3 August 2002. www.Mindbodyhealth.com/health-talk.

Hints and Tips for Climbing a Mountain. Intermountain Communications. 27 July 2002. www.intermountain.net/mthints.html.

The History of Candy. Candy USA. 4 August 2002. www.candyusa.org.

The History of Chocolate. Candy USA. 4 August 2002. www.candyuse.org.

The History of Christmas. Holidays on the Net. 4 August 2002. www.Holidays.net/Christmas/story.htm.

History of Diamonds. Costello's Jewelry. 4 September 2002. www.costellos.com au/diamonds/history.html.

The History of Diamonds. Diamonds of New York. 4 September 2002. www.Diamonds-ny.com/diamond-history.html.

History of Ice Cream. Here's the Scoop. 4 August 2002. www.heresthescoop.com/history.

The History of Ice Cream. Online Shopping.com. 4 August 2002. www.1-online-shopping.com/vip/food/ice-cream-history.htm.

The History of Toys and Games. The History Channel. 10 August 2002. www.Historychannel.com/exhibits/toys/crayons.html.

Hood, William Michael. *Yellow Jackets*. Clemson University. 12 September 2002. www.Hgic.Clemson.edu/factsheets/HGIC_rfln.htm.

How America Loves Chocolate. Candy USA. 4 August 2002. www.candyusa.org.

How to Change Your Car's Oil. PageWise. 18 November 2002. http://ksks.essortment.com./oilchanging_rvia.htm.

How to Change the Oil in Your Car. PageWise. 18 November 2002. http://meme.Essortment.com/carsoilchang_ruio.htm.

"How to Have Younger Skin." *Reader's Digest*. November 1994. 163+.

How to Play: Water Polo Rules. PageWise. 14 August 2002. http://sdsd.essortment.com/waterpolorules_rvnq.htm.

Hughes, Linda. *How to Kill Yellow Jackets*. PageWise. 12 September 2002. http://nenseeortment.com/howtokillyell_rfln.htm.

Hulley, P. Alexander. *Lanternfishes in General*. Iziko Museums of Cape Town. 2 October 2002. www.museums.org.za/sam/resource/marines/lanternhtm.

"Ice Cream Personalities." *Women Today*. 4 August 2002. www.Womentodaymagazine.com/foodcooking/icecreampersonality.html.

Information on HDL, LDL, VLDL, Cholesterol and Arteriosclerosis. Altruis Biomedical Network. 3 August 2002. www.Healthchecksystems.com.

International Tree Ring Data Bank Forum. University of Melbourne. 13 October 2002. www.civag.unimelb.edu.ua/~argnt/treeing/treefaq.html.

Interesting Fact About Chocolate and Its Effects. Dot Com. 21 August 2002. www.lovingchocolate.com/html/glossary.html.

An Introduction to Early Cinema. Early Cinema.com. 7 November 2002. www.Earlycinema.com/timeline/index.html.

Jackson, Donald W. "Planning Your Garden's Design." *Flower & Garden*. November 1999. 21 November 2002. www.findarticles.com.

Jansen, Paul A. *Insect Sting Allergy.* Emedicine. 12 September 2002. www.emedicine.com/aaem/topic269.htm.

Jerdee, Rebecca. "What Hue Are You?" *Better Homes and Gardens.* 3 August 2002. www.weprintcolor.com/colourmoodtest.html.

Jumper Cable Operating Instructions. Philatron International. 15 November 2002. www.philatron.com/tinytiger/instructions.html.

Kantrowitz, Barbara. "In Search of Sleep." *Newsweek.* 10 July 2002: 41.

Knight, J.D. "The Splendors of the Sea." *Sea and Sky.* 30 September 2002. www.seasky.org.

Landscape and Garden: Flower Gardening. Hometime Video Publishing, Inc. 21 November 2002. www.hometime.com/projects.howto/lawngrdn.htm.

Lawson, Nancy. Personal communication. 19 November 2002.

Lee, Stephen R. *Siberian Huskies.* Resources for the Canine Community. 4 August 2002. www.k9web.com/dogs-facqs/breeds/huskies.html.

Leiser, Judy. *Designing a Home Garden.* Paradox Productions, Inc. 21 November 2002. www.paradoxpm.com/homegarden.html.

Lewis, Jane Johnson. "Sacagawea: Guide to the West" *Women's History.* January 22, 2001. 3 November 2002. http://womenshistory.about.com/library/weekly.

Lewis, Kathleeen. *Light Descriptions/Requirements.* Lewis Gardens. 21 November 2002. www.lewisgardens.com/light.html.

Long, Caroline. "Health and Happiness—Does Chocolate Have It All Wrapped Up?" *International Food Information Service.* August 1999. 21 August 2002. www.ifis.con.uk/hottopics/chocolate.html.

Maas, Peter. *Miss Waldron's Red Colobus Monkey.* 23 July 2002. http://home.Conceptsfa.nl/~pmass/misswaldons-redcolobus.htm.

Maintenance. Automotive Information Center. 15 November 2002. www.autosite.com/garage/carcare/chklst.2asp.

Meador, Claudberta. *How to Check Tire Pressure.* PageWise. 18 November 2002. http://mt.essortment.com/checktirepress_reot.htm.

Miniature Poodle Dog. Dog Biz. 4 August 2002. www.dogbiz.com/dogs-grp6/poodle-min/poodle-mini.htm.

Mount Kilimanjaro. Peakware World Mountain Encyclopedia. 2 August 2002. www.peakware.com.

Mueller, John. Personal communications. 2 December 2002.

Native Peoples of North America. Cabrillo College. 18 September 2002. www.Cabrillo.cc.ca.us/~crsmith/mverde.html.

The Nature of Diamonds. San Diego Natural History Museum. 3 September 2002. www.sdnhm.org/exhibits/diamonds/facts.html.

Nissan Stanza Altima. Torrance, CA: Nissan, 1993.

Norris, Scott. "Reading Between the Lines." *Bioscience Online.* May 2001. 13 October 2002. www.findarticles.com.

Oliver, Vose, Sandifer, Murphy & Lee. *The Power of Eminent Domain.* OVSM&L. 10 September 2002. www.eminentdomainlaw.net/power.html.

Overpeck, Jonathan. *Understanding Past Drought Across the United States from Tree Rings.* National Climatic Data Center. 13 October 2002. www.ncdc.noaa.gov/ogp/papers/cook.html.

The Pan-Era Woman. National Association of Tribal Historic Preservation Officers. 17 September 2002. www.nathpo.org./Pan-era.html.

Parent, Margie. *How to Prepare Your Car for Winter*. PageWise. 18 November 2002. http://wy.essortment.com/carmaintenance_rayc.htm.

Patient Information on Allergic Reactions to Insect Stings. American Academy of Allergy and Immunology. 12 September 2002. www.aaai.org.

Paxton, John. *Classification, Diversity and Biology of Lanternfishes*. Australian Museum Online. 2 October 2002. www.amonline.net.au/fishes/about/research/paxton3.htm.

Player Positions & Descriptions. University of Richmond. 14 August 2002. http://geocities.com/spiderpolo/positions.html.

Poodle. American Kennel Club. 4 August 2002. www.akc.org/breeds/recBreeds/poodle.cfm.

A Preparedness Guide. National Weather Service. 24 July 2002. www.nws.Gov/om/brochures/tornado.htm.

Proclamation Establishing the Giant Sequoia National Monument. LLPOH. 13 October 2002. www.lipoh.org/sequoia.

Providing Homes and Hunting Grounds to Bird of Prey. Kansas City Power & Light. 3 December 2002. www.keplkids.com/tr_prey.html.

"Retire at 65? Better Change Your Plans." *Business Week Online*. 25 July 2002. http://aol.businessweek.com/magazine/content.

Rich, Candace. *The Fifties Web*. 1 August 2002. www.fiftiesweb.com.

Riley, Brendan. "Secrets of the Spirit Cave Man." *New Standard*. April 25, 1996. 17 September 2002. www.s-t.com/daily.

Sacagawea. PBS Online. 3 November 2002. www.pbs.org/lewisandclark/inside/saca.html.

"Scientists Win Kennewick Man Ruling." *Tri City Herald*. August 31, 2002. 16 September 2002. http://kennewick-man.com/news/083102.html.

Shin Splints. All Running Shoes. 4 December 2002. www.allrunningshoes.com/shinsplints.html.

"Shinsplints Are a Pain in the Tibialis." *Men's Fitness*. August 2002. 4 December 2002. www.findarticles.com.

Siberian Husky. American Kennel Club. 4 August 2002. www.akc.org/breeds/recbreeds/sibhusk.cfm.

Siberian Husky. Dog Biz. 4 August 2002. www.dogbiz.com/dogs-grp3/siberian/siberian.htm.

Silva, Samantha. "A Famous Skeleton Returns to the Earth." *High Country News*. March 8, 1993. 20 September 2002. www.hen.org/1993/mar08/dir/lead.html.

Skin Health. iVillage. 20 July 2002. www.ivillagehealth.com/library.

So You Wanna Improve Your Table Manners? Soyouwanna.com. 4 December 2002. www.soyouwanna.com/site/syws/tablemanners/tablemanners.html.

"Spirit Cave Man Timeline." *Reno Gazette Journal*. August 16, 2000. 17 September 2002. www.rgj.com/news/stories/news.

Starbuck, Christopher J. *Making and Using Compost*. University of Missouri. 18 November 2002. http://muextension.missouri.edu/splor/agguides/hort/g06956.htm.

Steckel, Mark. *Shin Splints*. Wellington Chiropractic. 4 December 2002. www.Spinalhealth.net/inj-shin.html.

Sterling, Ian, ed. *Bears, Majestic Creatures of the Wild*. Emmaus, PA, 1993. Ed. Jim Tomlin. The International Association for Bear Research and Management. www.bearbiology.com/bbdesc.html.

Stiles, Lori. *Scientists, Volunteers Seek Tree Rings to Lengthen Ancient Bristlecone Record*. University of Arizona. 13 October 2002. http://opi.arizona.edu/cgi-bin/WebObjects.

Stiles, Lori. *UA Scientist Discovered Earth's Oldest Living Trees 50 Years Ago*. University of Arizona. 13 October 2002. http://opi.arizona.edu/cgi-bin/WebObjects.

Stress Management. Georgia Reproductive Specialists. 14 August 2002. www.ivf.com/stress.html.

Technology: Baseball Design. Worth Sports. 13 November 2002. www.worthsports.com/technology/balldesign.html.

"Tips for Driving in Snow and Ice." *Lubbock Avalanche-Journal*. 2 December 2002. http://lubbock.online.com/news.

Tips for Healthy Hair. iVillage. 24 November 2002. www.ivillage.com/dietfeatures/herbs.

Tips for Healthy Hair. Womensforum.com. 24 November 2002. www.thefamilycorner.com/justforyou/health/haircare.shtml.

Top Ten Attractions. Yellowstone.Net. 23 July 2003. www.yellowstone.net/topic.htm.

Toussaint Chabonneau. PBS Online. 3 November 2002. www.pbs.org/Lewisandclark/tchar.html.

Trail of a Hundred Giants. KernValley.com. 31 October 2002. www.kernvalley.com/news/trail100.htm.

"Tree Rings Reveal Cycle of Global Warming." *CBS News*. March 22, 2002. 13 October 2002. www.cbc.ca/stories/2002/03.

Tynes, Mary J. *Step-By-Step Instructions to Build a Compost Pile*. Mastercomposter.com. 18 November 2002. www.mastercomposster.com/pile/advbuild.html.

Types of Coffee Beans. PageWise. 10 September 2002. www.vava.essortment.com/typesofcoffee_rhit.htm.

Types of Investments. Personal Money Management. 14 August 2002. www.e-personal-money-management.com/typesinvest.html.

Understanding How Colour Affects Your Mood. Reprotech Digital Media Services. 3 August 2002. www.weprintcolour.com/colourmoodtest.phtml.

"Understanding Sleep." *Talk About Sleep*. 19 August 2002. www.edweek.org/ew/newstory.cfm.

USGS Investigates West Nile Virus, Steps Up Bird Surveillance. U.S. Department of the Interior. 29 July 2002. www.usgs.gov/wnvfactsheet.html.

Vinson Massif. Peakware World Encyclopedia. 2 August 2002. www.peakware.com.

Walker, Brad. "The Stretching & Sports Injury Newsletter." *The Stretching Handbook*. 4 December 2002. www.thestretchinghandbook.com/archives/shin-splints.htm.

West Nile Virus. Centers for Disease Control and Prevention. 29 July 2002. http://dep.org/html/Wn.html.

West Nile Virus Maps—2002. U.S. Department of the Interior. 29 July 2002. http://cindi/sugs.gov/hazard/event/west_nile/west_nile.html.

What Is a Diamond? Diamond Education & Information Centre. 4 September 2002. www.diamonds.org/education/historye.html.

What Is the Myer-Briggs Type Indicator? Association for Psychological Type. 2 August 2002. www.aptcentral.org/aptmbtiw.htm.

What Is Your Personality Type? Advisor Team. 2 August 2002. www.advisorteam.com/keirsey.

Who Was First? Cabrillo College. 17 September 2002. www.cabrillo.cc.ca.us/~crsmith/prince.html.

Wilson, James D. and John Meyer. *Who Needs Cliffs?* Missouri Department of Conservation. 3 December 2002. www.conservation.state.mo.us/conmag/1999/01/4.html.

World's Most Famous Diamonds. Love Story Diamonds. 3 September 2002. www.love-story.com.

Yahnke, Robert. *Cinema History.* University of Minnesota. 7 November 2002. www.genumn.edu/faculty_staff/yanhke/film/cinema1.htm.

Yellow Jacket Wasp. Buffalo Exterminating Company. 12 September 2002. www.buffaloexterminating.com/yellow.html.

Yellowstone National Park. National Park Service. 23 July 2002. www.nps.gov/yell.

Yosemite National Park. National Park Service. 23 July 2003. www.nps.gov/yose.

Yosemite National Park Information Page. National Park Service. 23 July 2002. www.yosemite.national-park.com/info.htm.

Young, Richard M. *Sacagawea.* SacagaweaHome.com. 3 November 2002. www.sacajaweahome.com/Stories.htm.

Zerbes, M. *Largest Earthquakes in the United States.* U.S. National Earthquake Information Center. 27 July 2002. http://neic.usgs.gov/equlists/USA/1964_03.

Share Your Bright Ideas

We want to hear from you!

Your name_____Date_____

School name_____

School address_____

City _____State_____Zip_____Phone number (_____)_____

Grade level(s) taught_____Subject area(s) taught_____

Where did you purchase this publication?_____

In what month do you purchase a majority of your supplements?_____

What moneys were used to purchase this product?

____School supplemental budget   ____Federal/state funding   ____Personal

Please "grade" this Walch publication in the following areas:

	A	B	C	D
Quality of service you received when purchasing	A	B	C	D
Ease of use	A	B	C	D
Quality of content	A	B	C	D
Page layout	A	B	C	D
Organization of material	A	B	C	D
Suitability for grade level	A	B	C	D
Instructional value	A	B	C	D

COMMENTS:_____

_____

What specific supplemental materials would help you meet your current—or future—instructional needs?

_____

Have you used other Walch publications? If so, which ones?_____

May we use your comments in upcoming communications?   ____Yes   ____No

Please **FAX** this completed form to **888-991-5755**, or mail it to

Customer Service, J. Weston Walch, Publisher, P. O. Box 658, Portland, ME 04104-0658

We will send you a **FREE GIFT** in appreciation of your feedback. **THANK YOU!**